CHILDREN'S HOME MUSICAL EXPERIENCES ACROSS THE WORLD

COUNTERPOINTS: MUSIC AND EDUCATION

Estelle R. Jorgensen, *editor*

CHILDREN'S HOME MUSICAL EXPERIENCES ACROSS THE WORLD

Edited by Beatriz Ilari and Susan Young

Indiana University Press

Bloomington and Indianapolis

This book is a publication of

Indiana University Press
Office of Scholarly Publishing
Herman B Wells Library 350
1320 East 10th Street
Bloomington, Indiana 47405 USA

iupress.indiana.edu

♾ The paper used in this publication meets the minimum requirements of the American National Standard for Information Sciences—Permanence of Paper for Printed Library Materials, ANSI Z39.48-1992.

Manufactured in the United States of America

Library of Congress Cataloging-in-Publication Data

Names: Ilari, Beatriz Senoi, editor. | Young, Susan, editor.
Title: Children's home musical experiences across the world / edited by Beatriz Ilari and Susan Young.
Description: Bloomington : Indiana University Press, 2016. | Series: Counterpoints : music and education | Includes bibliographical references and index.
Identifiers: LCCN 2016018113 (print) | LCCN 2016020661 (ebook) | ISBN 9780253022004 (cloth : alk. paper) | ISBN 9780253022103 (pbk. : alk. paper) | ISBN 9780253022172 (ebook)
Subjects: LCSH: Music—Instruction and study—Cross-cultural studies. | Home schooling. | Music in the home.
Classification: LCC MT1 .C5333 2016 (print) | LCC MT1 (ebook) | DDC 780.83/4—dc23
LC record available at https://lccn.loc.gov/2016018113

1 2 3 4 5 21 20 19 18 17 16

We dedicate this book to the children in our lives:
Alice, Charlie, Edward, Harry, Isabella, and Mitchell.

Contents

Acknowledgments

First and foremost we would like to thank all children and families whose lives are portrayed in this book. In different parts of the world, busy families with seven-year-olds welcomed our research team members into their lives. They showed us their homes, their gardens, their favorite objects, and their pets, while we sipped juice, coffee or tea. They sang favorite tunes, danced, shared their compositions, musical toys, and electronic devices in our presence. They also laughed, frowned, smiled, and showed concern as they answered some of our most intriguing questions. Some even shared secrets, anxieties, and deepest fears with us. This book is the result of a collective effort to describe, interpret, and make sense of what we have experienced as we entered the homes and lives of these remarkable families. If it were not for their willingness to share their ideas and experiences with us, this book would never have been written.

The feedback received from fellow scholars was of ultimate importance for the refinement of our work over time. We are especially grateful to Estelle Jorgensen for her encouragement when we began to imagine an edited book on the MyPlace, MyMusic research project. Our gratitude is extended to Carlos Abril and Joanne Rutkowski, who have spent a considerable amount of their time immersed in our manuscript. They offered constructive criticisms and insightful recommendations that have helped to strengthen the arguments laid out in this book. Raina Polivka, Darja Malcolm-Clarke and the entire team at Indiana University Press have provided much guidance and support throughout the publication process, which certainly made our work smoother.

A heartfelt thank you goes out to Marcel Soleda for his technical assistance and support with the assemblage of the wiki. We also thank Bettina Schouw and African Cream Music for granting us permission to publish the score for "Hambo Lala" that appears in chapter 8, and Lydio Roberto for allowing us to publish the score for "Sabiá" in chapter 3. We are also grateful to the families in Spain, Kenya, and South Africa for giving us permission to publish pictures of their children.

We are indebted to the entire MyPlace, MyMusic research team. This extraordinary group of researchers from different corners of the world worked collaboratively for several years to make this project come to life. We thank Jèssica Pérez-Moreno who served as "wiki coordinator" and ensured that all materials were received and made available to all. Furthermore, we would like to express our sincere gratitude to Anna Rita Addessi and Francesca Minigher in Italy, Sven-Erik Holgersen in Denmark, Jennifer Leu in Taiwan, and José Retra in the

Netherlands. Although they did not contribute chapters to this volume, their roles in the project were equally important. We sincerely hope to have done justice to the invaluable data that they have collected, which are thoroughly discussed here.

Finally, we thank our family members and friends (Lisi Zeni) for their encouragement and unfailing support during the preparation of this volume.

CHILDREN'S HOME MUSICAL EXPERIENCES ACROSS THE WORLD

Introduction

MyPlace, MyMusic: Children's Home Musical Experiences Across the World

Beatriz Ilari and Susan Young

Framed predominantly by methods and theories from developmental psychology and usually with the school as a main locus, research on children's music education has at times endorsed the view of music as a "thing" to be learned by specific social and cultural groups. Music education research has also embraced, for the most part, the logic that music learning and development occur in universal stages, moving in a somewhat linear fashion from simple to complex with adult abilities as the endpoint, and with little exploration of contextual issues. This is made evident by the large volume of controlled studies on the musical skills and behaviors of children and adults, which still dominates music education research to date. As important as they are, these works provide a partial view of music learning and development in childhood. In recent years, however, efforts have been made to understand how and why humans engage with music in everyday life and the ways in which these experiences relate to music teaching and learning. Seminal works in the social psychology of music (e.g., Clarke, Dibben, and Pitts, 2008; Hargreaves and North, 1998; North and Hargreaves, 2008), sociology of music and music education (DeNora, 2000; Small, 1998; Wright, 2010), ethnomusicology (e.g., Turino, 2006), and more recently, cultural psychology (Barrett, 2011), have been particularly important in this regard. Social psychologists and sociologists, for example, have called our attention to the fact that music is, above all, a social endeavour (Hargreaves and North, 1998; Small, 1998). Their works remind us that music learning is directly linked to human interactions and to the ways that diverse social groups view and differentiate humans based on age, sex and gender, race, religion, ethnicity, and so on (e.g., Green, 1997; O'Neill, 1997). Likewise, ethnomusicologists, anthropologists, and cultural psychologists have problematized how cultural beliefs, values, and practices shape human belief systems, cognition, and action (Barrett, 2011; Campbell, 2002; Turino, 2006), suggesting that music learning is intimately linked to the many cultures and subcultures that surround the individual. It is significant that these works not only highlight the role that different contexts play in musical experiences but also bring attention to local, global, and *glocal* or "think globally, act locally" (Himonides, 2012, p. 449) aspects of music, musical engagement, and learning. It follows, then, that music is a pervasive everyday life phenomenon that exists in various forms and takes on different meanings across and within cultures (see Young, 2015). Musical engagement, learning, and development not only are by-products of human abilities to perceive and process musical sounds but also are directly linked to issues of agency, identity, ethnicity, belief systems, and social and cultural values, to name a few.

A contextualized and integrated view of music, musical engagement, and learning is consistent with recent theorizing in the field of Childhood Studies. A prolific academic field that draws from a wide range of disciplines such as anthropology, sociology, history, public policy, law, and education, Childhood Studies focuses on childhood as a special social category and calls into question conventional concepts related to children and childhood (James, Jenks, and Prout, 1998). As described in the *Oxford Bibliographies* on "Childhood Studies": "Contemporary Childhood Studies is also characterized by its insistence on the need for children themselves to be understood as the best informants of their own lives. Scholars therefore look at children's own cultures, meanings and the ways in which they attempt to change their lives and the lives of adults around them" (Childhood Studies, p. 1). Hedegaard, Aronsson, Højholt, and Ulvik (2012) have also contended that a main challenge for researchers today is to "present empirical studies of child development that involve studies of children and children's development, situated across different settings and activities" (p. vii).

This relatively new approach to music engagement and learning, to which we devote serious attention in chapter 1, has framed a small number of recent works concerning children (e.g., Dean, 2015; Kerchner and Abril, 2009; Lum, 2008; St. John, 2009; Young, 2012a; Young and Ilari, 2012). Arguably, the adoption of Childhood Studies as a theoretical stance to study children's musical engagement allows for a more holistic view of music making. Researchers are now attempting to bring out children's voices by paying much attention to contextual issues while resisting the temptation to universalize experiences (Kanellopoulos, 2010, p. 128). A view of children's musical engagement and learning oriented by Childhood Studies also aligns with the idea of children as competent agents who navigate diverse communities of practice (Barrett, 2005; Wenger, 1999). Through participation in the sociocultural activities of everyday life (Rogoff, 2003) and in a specific point in history, children not only learn music, but they develop and construct identities around it.

Music in Homes with Young Children

Increasingly children in many societies spend a considerable amount of time at home as opposed to playing in the streets or surrounding neighborhoods, due in part to a widespread and ever growing social perception of risk associated with these spaces (Malone, 2007). At the same time, there has been an increase and intensification of home musical activities, which are directly linked to the rapid advancements in digital technologies and access to them by adults and children alike. Given that children learn music through participation in the daily activities of their surroundings from very early on (Young and Ilari, 2012), it seems logical to consider the home as both a central (Lamont, 2008) and an optimal site to investigate musical engagement and learning in childhood. This orientation toward the home—as opposed to the school or other communal space—as a site for studying children's musicking (Small, 1998) and learning is consistent with developments in related fields. On that note, anthropological research has led toward the turning of attention to childhood in "near" rather than "faraway" places (Lancy, 2008), and this trend has been and continues to be followed by scholars from other fields (e.g., Tudge, 2008).

While interest in the topic of children's musical studies in the home in the developed world is arguably not new (e.g., Atterbury and Silcox, 1993; Brand, 1986), an inherent problem in this type of investigation lies in issues of privacy and access. Conducting research in homes is difficult because entering someone's home also means entering the private space of the family with its intricate web of relationships, habits, schedules, and meanings. In other words, a fair amount of disruption takes place once observers and recording devices are placed in a home. Furthermore, parenting and family life are dynamic and changing as a consequence of children's development and growth as well as social, cultural, and political forces (Alwin, 2003). So, even when the door of a home is opened for research purposes, the view that emerges is likely to be partial and time-sensitive.

The home was a popular research site, particularly between the 1960s and 1980s, when major concerns were raised about the influence of the environment in which children lived on their overall development. During that time, scholars were especially interested in relationships between the home environment and children's development in several areas, especially academic achievement. Links were established between environmental factors such as parents' use of rewards, parental support and intellectual stimulation of children, language use in homes with children of varied ages, and children's cognitive abilities (see Brand, 1986). Analogously, some positive correlations were also found between environmental factors such as concert attendance, provision of musical materials, and parental support and school-age children's musical and extramusical abilities (Brand,

1986; Zdzinski, 1996). A recent study carried out in Australia extended the implications of these and similar findings, suggesting that the frequency of home-shared musical experiences in toddlerhood is positively associated with numeracy, prosociality, and attention in preschoolers (Williams, Barrett, Welch, Abad, and Broughton, 2015).

Aside from correlational research, descriptive works have also been carried out. Many studies on home musical experiences have focused on families with small children. This is understandable, given the large amount of time that is usually spent in the home as well as the demands placed on parents, particularly in the first years of life when children need constant supervision and care. Unsurprisingly, musical parenting, or the beliefs, values, attitudes, and behaviors of parents toward their children's musical experiences, has been at the heart of multiple investigations. Surveys and interview data have provided glimpses into parental beliefs and values concerning music and musical behaviors of small children in the home (e.g., Custodero and Johnson-Green, 2003; DeVries, 2009; Ilari, 2005; Ilari, Moura, and Bourscheidt, 2011; Mehr, 2014; Young, 2008). Other studies have relied on interviews and observations of parents and children in the home to uncover parental beliefs, forms of musical engagement during musical play, and parent–child relationships regarding instrumental experiences and practicing habits of young performers (Adachi, 2008; Addessi, 2009; Barrett, 2005, 2009; Palheiros and Hargreaves, 2001; Creech, 2009; Custodero, 2006; Davidson, Howe, Moore, and Sloboda, 1996; Dean, 2015; Ilari and Chitwood, 2016; Kelley and Sutton-Smith, 1987; Lum, 2008; McPherson, 2009; Mualem and Klein, 2011; Young and Gillen, 2011).

Taken together, these works provide a window into the rich musical worlds that exist in the privacy of the home. Music appears to be alive and well—to some extent—in homes with children under the age of seven through singing, listening, and performing. Parents, siblings and extended kin, friends and community members are important sources of musical stimulation. Repertoires and practices vary across age and cultural groups, yet some common elements among them include the use of an affective singing mode when singing to babies and toddlers and a gradual increase of pop tunes heard in the household as children develop and grow in culture. Thus, an intricate web of parental beliefs and attitudes toward music, musical affordances in the home, cultural values, and the mass media play a considerable role in children's home musical experiences. But, as informative as they are, these studies paint only a partial picture. There is still much more to be uncovered. How social class, ethnicity and culture, the mass media, and global issues influence the home musical experiences of middle-class children around the world, particularly those who are not necessarily enrolled in formal music classes, remains elusive (see Young, 2012b). The extent to which digital technologies permeate home musicking of today's children and the experiences resulting from such interactions are also unclear. This is especially true regarding musical engagement in the "late years" of early childhood (e.g., age seven).[1] The late years of early childhood have been somewhat neglected by early childhood music educators, who have directed their attention mainly to babies and preschoolers. Yet it is around the time when children transition between the early years and compulsory schooling that they gradually move from the "institutional charge" of the family to a combined social arrangement that includes shared responsibilities and influences from family, school, and the community at large (Garcia Coll and Marks, 2009). How children from different social and cultural groups navigate these different "worlds" or communities of practice (Wenger, 1999), and how the latter influence their musical engagement, learning, and development needs to be further explored.

It is also enticing to study musical engagement in homes of seven-year-olds in view of the general idea that it differs considerably from what happens in formal learning contexts, such as schools and conservatories (Gaunt, 2005; Palheiros and Hargreaves, 2001). As Hedegaard (2012) has contended, on a social level children "meet different types of demands in home activity settings" (p. 55), and also create demands for their family members. On a personal level, children experience a sense of control when engaging with music in the home, and the motivations behind these experiences tend to be more related to fruition and leisure than to explicit/deliberate forms of learning that are typically found in schooling (Palheiros and Hargreaves, 2001). Yet, what happens musically in the home is likely to be related—to some degree—to what happens musically in school and vice versa (see Hedegaard, 2012). As children negotiate their participation in these different communities of practice, they develop and construct identities. Thus, knowledge of children's musical engagement in the home has direct implications for music education. The repertoires that children engage with, the means for doing so, and their relationships to gender, schooling, family values, and parental expectations offer interesting insights into childhood and musical development. This is particularly valuable in our current times of globalization, constant cultural exchanges, and rapid technological developments.

MyPlace, MyMusic: A Collective Research Project

Based on a collective research project carried out by fourteen members of the International Society for Music Education–Early Childhood Commission and their graduate students, this book brings together a fresh perspective on home musical activities of middle-class seven-year-olds in diverse countries. The aim of this book is to disseminate and discuss findings from the research project, in order to motivate debate about the types of everyday home-based musical activities in which seven-year-old children in internationally diverse locations are typically involved, their partners in those activities, the roles taken, where, why, and with what resources, major influences, and the meanings associated with them.

A unique aspect of this project is its collective and collaborative nature. Each research team member contributed one set of data from their location. Research team members followed a common protocol, which is presented in detail below, and then shared data with the group by means of a wiki (see chapter 2). Thus, each participant had access to a larger and more internationally diverse body of data than they would have been able to achieve single-handedly. Although some analyses proceeded along collaboratively agreed-on lines of inquiry, individual researchers also had opportunities to follow their own lines of interest.

The central research questions framing this collective research project were:

- What is the nature and range of home musical activities of middle-class, seven-year-olds in diverse locations across the world?
- What and who are the major influences in children's musical engagements in the home?
- What do home musical experiences mean for children, their families, and communities?

Project Aims

On a theoretical level, the project is aimed at addressing some important gaps found in the literature. First, we decided to gather information on music in the home in the late years of early childhood, which coincide with the early years of middle childhood (Young, 2012b), a period of life that has received little attention from the scholarly community. As noted, although many have acknowledged the importance of the home environment in children's musicking (Small, 1998), studies centering on home musical experiences of children have focused predominantly on the experiences of babies, toddlers, and preschoolers (e.g., Custodero and Johnson-Green, 2001; Ilari, 2005; Young, 2008), and have said little about slightly older children. Second, we followed Tudge's (2008) lead concerning the need to address the relative absence of cultural work that considers heterogeneity within a given society or social group as a result of social class, ethnicity, and race. This absence is quite problematic, especially in music education research, which has tended to consider these issues as independent variables. We discuss these issues in more depth in chapter 1, but for now, it suffices to say that we are concerned about the need to adopt a culturally bound view of musical participation in childhood (Young and Ilari, 2012). But instead of taking a strictly cross-cultural perspective, in which predetermined ideas are usually tested in different cultural contexts, we observed and described children in their homes first, to then set the individual "cases" side by side. Through this process, we arrived at broader ideas that emerged through an inductive process of interpretation of data from diverse locations (Creswell, 2011). The data from individual children were then juxtaposed (Rogoff, 2003), thus leaving much room for similarities and regularities to emerge. In other words, we prioritized the collection of many rich examples of children's musical lives, which could then be scrutinized by a team of experienced researchers who brought in a wide range of different analytical approaches and perspectives.

Thus, while we used this comparative process, we were also concerned about maintaining qualitative methodology in which themes and patterns typically emerge from the data. Young (2012b, p. 9) has argued elsewhere that this was "more a process of reflective awareness than systematic analysis; more a question of generating new meanings and understandings, which are judged in terms of their usefulness and plausibility, than accessing some assumed, transparent realities." Unsurprisingly, this entire process transformed the dialogue between members of the research team, who themselves represented different backgrounds, ethnicities, cultural groups, and geographical areas, into an essential means for both generating and analyzing data (see Young, 2012b). That is, each individual researcher had the opportunity to analyze his or her own local data, while examining data collected by others in different parts of the world. Our data were also analyzed in terms of recent dichotomies such as the global and the local, the majority and the minority worlds (see chapter 1), and so forth, which have been central to social and education research (e.g., Fleer, Hedegaard, and Tudge, 2009), but, to our knowledge, are yet to be fully embraced by music education scholars.

On a more specific note, the project set out a number of aims as described by Young (2012b):

- To expand accounts of children's musical development by collecting data on children's musical practices from heterogeneous contexts;
- To expand knowledge of the everyday home music experiences of 7-year-old children in internationally diverse locations;
- To collect information on the resources for music in the home with particular attention to technological devices, and to expand understanding of how technology is influencing the range and nature of musical engagement for young children in the home;
- To collect information on the media resources for music in the home, with particular attention to children's popular culture, and to expand understanding of how popular culture is influencing the range and nature of musical activity for young children in the home;
- To collect information on any local musical traditions (with particular attention to traditions associated with religious practices) that may impact on the range and nature of musical practice for young children in the home;

- To build a database of 7-year-olds from internationally diverse locations singing a song of their own choice;
- To build a database of a "typical week of music" for the 7-year-olds.

Each researcher addressed these aims to a broader or narrower extent.

Methods

A common research protocol designed by the editors of this volume was used in the project. Instead of being overly prescriptive, the research protocol was designed with some flexibility to accommodate cultural variances. In designing the protocol, it was important to be mindful that our research team members came from different countries, where different research traditions and values predominate. Therefore, it was vital to provide some flexibility in the research protocol, so that individual researchers could adjust it as they saw fit and in accordance with each local culture. An overly prescriptive protocol would invariably center on one research orientation and probably result in a more Euro-American perspective than desired. Furthermore, it might have closed some windows of opportunity for learning about uncharted aspects of the musical lives of participating children from otherwise underresearched parts of the world (Young, 2012b). Thus, instead of viewing differences as flaws or problems, our research team welcomed emergent differences because we understood them to be an integral and important part of the interpretive process (see Eisner, 2002).

Each research team member recruited one or two, seven-year-olds (preferably two, a boy and a girl) from the local community. Children were exactly seven years old at the time of the home visit and were considered to be thriving according to local standards. Furthermore, each child had to be a full member of an indigenous local population or at least third-generation settlers in the country, and similar to the researcher/fieldworker in ethnicity and social-class standing (i.e., middle class). Given that definitions of ethnicity and social class vary considerably across cultures and countries, individual researchers were instructed to follow local definitions and guidelines during recruitment. We also requested that researchers recruit children who would be confident and competent in communicating independently with an adult fieldworker. Since our research method required that children do a "show and tell" of their musical resources and activities at home, it seemed sensible to include this criterion (Young, 2012b).

Once researchers had located their participants, a home visit of one to two hours was arranged, usually by telephone, at the family's convenience. On arrival at the home, the researcher/fieldworker briefly explained the purpose of the research project and its procedures, and asked parents to sign consent forms. Next, children and parents were interviewed informally about music in their daily lives. In some families, children were interviewed in the presence of one parent or both parents. In others, parents and children were interviewed separately. As mentioned

Table 0.1. Weekly schedule of children's typical musical activities, completed by parents during the home visit.
Instruction: Please complete the grid for a typical week of music. Not every box needs an insertion.

	Early morning (before school)	Morning	Afternoon	Early Evening	Late Evening/ Bedtime
Monday					
Tuesday					
Wednesday					
Thursday					
Friday					
Saturday					
Sunday					

earlier, during the home visit, children were asked to do a "show and tell" of any musical items that they deemed important, including toys, instruments, and technological gadgets. We noticed that some children were also very eager to perform on different musical instruments for the researcher/fieldworker. Children were also asked to sing one or more favorite songs "for the record." Interviews, song renditions, and "show and tell" sessions were either videotaped or audiotaped, depending on parental agreement. Parents were asked to fill out a weekly schedule concerning children's regular musical activities in a typical week (see Table 0.1).

Each researcher/fieldworker had collected a large amount of data on leaving individual homes. Apart from the recorded interviews, "show and tell" video, and children's sung renditions, researchers also made careful photographic documentation of the homes and their locations and wrote detailed notes concerning the surrounding area/neighborhoods. Several researchers drew house plans, described the local climate and surrounding landscape, and made a list of musical resources in the home and their locations within it, as well as collected detailed information regarding consumption of media, technology, and popular culture. Researchers and fieldworkers also took notes on family configuration (i.e., descriptions of family members, their age, occupation, etc.), musical interests and background, and social, cultural, or religious musical traditions that families commonly engaged in or deemed relevant.

Once all data were collected, the next step involved transcribing interviews and, in most cases, translating them from a wide range of languages (e.g., Hebrew, Danish, Dutch, Italian, and Brazilian Portuguese) into English, the lingua franca of the project. Individual researchers were then asked to fill out a summary of their data using a structured template (Table 0.2). This was an important step in the organization of data for subsequent dissemination and interpretation.

Table 0.2. Structured template summarizing children's background and main data points gathered during home visits. Created by Theano Koutsoupidou.

Child's ID (pseudonym)
Date of birth:
Place of birth:
Place of residence:
Ethnicity:
Mother tongue:
Religion (if any):
Comments:

Family
Ethnicity:
Mother's occupation:
Fathers' occupation:
Siblings (if any):
Regular visits by:
Comments:

School
Type of School:
Information about schooling in child's home country:
Hours attending:
Classmates' ethnicity:
Music lesson:
Other music activities at school:

The visit
Date of visit / Comments:

Child's musical interests
Child's personality
Videos
Field notes and comments
Permission and consent
Other documents

Next, structured templates, interview transcriptions (translated when necessary), and other materials were sent to a central researcher, who became responsible for organizing and disseminating information by means of the wiki (see Pérez-Moreno, chapter 2, this volume). Because the construction of the wiki, including its rationale and actual functioning is fully described in the next chapter, we now turn to a brief comment about the child participants, before introducing the remaining chapters of the book.

A Brief Comment about the Child Participants

Seventeen children in twelve different countries took part in the project. All the project participants were thriving, in good health, and attending regular schools. This sample of children was one of convenience (Creswell, 2011), which means that some limitations are associated with our findings.[2] Still, it was also reassuring to witness how our entrance into children's lifeworlds revealed a wide range of both convergences and divergences in their experiences, values, and beliefs (Gillen and Cameron, 2010; Tudge, 2008), including where music was concerned. Children's musical worlds were neither static nor stereotyped. They were musical worlds of school, family, peers, community, the media and commerce, as well as private and public ones. "Our" children seemed to navigate well in these different (and at times contrasting) worlds. Yet they all had to learn to articulate their musical activities according to different situations. Some children learned music within the auspices of their communities; others were enrolled in a wide range of extracurricular musical activities, including private and group lessons led by experts. Participating children were also surrounded—to some extent—by worlds of media, technology, and popular culture, which dictated many of their musical experiences and exchanges. They consumed music in a wide range of ways, confirming the existence of multiple musical childhoods (see Young, chapter 1, this volume). These were, in turn, influenced by several factors, including gender and identity (Andang'o and Pacheco, chapter 4, this volume) ethnicity, parental beliefs and values (Koutsoupidou, chapter 5, this volume), and social class (Ilari, chapter 6, this volume), to name a few. A short summary of children's musical lives is presented in Table 0.3 at the end of this chapter. Rather than presenting a detailed description and subjective interpretation of each individual child and his/her families, we invite readers to construct these as they read through the chapters. In doing so we not only remain true to the interpretive process of qualitative research but also provide readers with the opportunity to reinterpret what our eyes, ears, hearts, and minds perceived in the process of analyzing data for this project.

Home Musical Experiences of Seven-Year-Olds: Chapter Descriptions

As we were putting this volume together, we wondered about the best way to disseminate our findings. As early childhood music education researchers working at what many would consider "the margins" (i.e., with slightly "older" children), we faced some dilemmas. Should we provide a rather descriptive account of what we witnessed in the homes? Might we attempt to connect and contrast what we witnessed in the homes in light of current theorizing in cultural studies? Or should we strive to make connections with the school environment, which has been the most common site of music education research? We posed these questions to our research team members early on. They were asked to construct their abstracts (and later their chapters) based on some aspect of the data. Research team members were free to explore any themes or ideas that they deemed interesting, but without losing site of a strong, underlying theoretical framework in which to base their interpretation of data, particularly the works of Gillen and Cameron (2010), Rogoff (2003), Small (1998), and Tudge (2008). This reflective exercise resulted in nine very different chapters, which we believe do justice to the uniqueness of our methodology and richness of data and also expand them in many directions.

The chapters were organized in three main sections. The first section includes descriptions of the theoretical frameworks and methodology of the project as a whole. In chapter 1, Susan Young of the University of Exeter in the United Kingdom provides an in-depth discussion concerning the "new" orientation to the study of children's musical engagement and learning in everyday life. She begins her chapter with a critique of the current state of affairs of music education research involving children, which is still heavily dominated by psychology and its universal developmental models. Young proposes a new look at children's musical engagement, centered on theoretical underpinnings from Childhood Studies. This interdisciplinary field of inquiry challenges some taken-for-granted concepts that involve the child, childhood, and development, and examines them in light of sociological, anthropological, and historical sources. Childhood Studies also urges researchers to conceptualize "children as being" rather than "children as becoming" (James, Jenks, and Prout, 1998). Young reexamines several of these taken-for-granted concepts associated with children's musical experiences, in particular, the concept of musical childhood, which is often conceptualized as universal in music education research. She argues against the universality of this concept, and proposes that we speak of musical childhoods, in the plural. Her argument is corroborated by innumerable examples from the MyPlace, MyMusic data set, which are described in subsequent chapters.

In chapter 2, Jèssica Pérez-Moreno of the Universitat Autònoma de Barcelona in Spain describes the construction of the wiki that was used as means for the researchers to exchange data sets. She was the "central researcher" described earlier, or, the person who became responsible for putting together the wiki, under the direct supervision of Susan Young. In her chapter, theories from computer science, new technologies, and media are used to sustain the argument that technology can, indeed, function as a catalyst for collaborative research. Readers will certainly draw many implications for future collaborative research in music education and related areas. These two chapters lay the foundation enabling readers to understand the subsequent chapters that center on selected subsets of the data.

Section II is composed of four chapters based on thematic interpretations of the collected data. Claudia Gluschankof of the Levinsky College of Education in Israel is the author of chapter 3. Theories from Childhood Studies and the Sociology of Childhood guide her analysis of children's musical engagements in the home and the relationship of these engagements with public and private—or secret—spheres of life. Gluschankof also brings to light an important discussion on children's cultures and musical cultures. As she explains, such conceptions emerge in the patterns of activities, behaviors, and interactions of child participants (see Gillen and Cameron, 2010). Gluschankof describes private and secret musical worlds, and musical cultures, but at the same time leaves room for readers to reinterpret the data. The implications for music education are obviously many.

Written by Elizabeth Andang'o of Kenyatta University, Kenya, and Caroline Brendel Pacheco of the Federal University of Paraíba, Brazil, chapter 4 tackles the issue of gendered meanings in children's musical engagements in the home and how these engagements shape identity. The study of gender and gendered meanings associated with musical experiences has received considerable attention from music sociologists, but less so from music education researchers. Andang'o and Pacheco bring to light the multifaceted nature of gendered meanings in music, by examining multiple sources of influence including the family and the surrounding cultures. Theories and data are interwoven in the chapter, and some certainties are "troubled," as in the case of the stereotyping of musical instruments (Colley, Mulhern, Relton, and Shafi, 2008), an area that has been quite well-established in Anglo- and Eurocentric research circles.

In chapter 5, Theano Koutsoupidou of the Mediterranean College in Athens, Greece, discusses musical parenting in six participating families. Koutsoupidou constructs her theoretical framework by relying on existing literature in both music psychology and music education (e.g., McPherson, 2009; Sichivitsa, 2007) to make sense of parental interview data. Emerging categories include parents' background, musical appreciation, musical provision for their children, and support for learning, and Koutsoupidou is careful to bring out parental voices throughout the text. At least two important ideas derive from her chapter. First, parents appear to be highly invested in nurturing their children's musical lives, regardless of their own musical values (e.g., performance versus enjoyment) and where and how they live their lives. Second, the nurturance of a musical child is a complex process, with families, cultures, and surrounding environments

Table 0.3. Descriptions of child participants, their family members and sources of musical stimulation in the home. Based on Ilari (2013).

Country	Child (pseudonym and sex)	Ethnicity, nationality, cultural background, religion	Interviewees	Other family members (not interviewed)
Brazil (1)	Giovanna (Girl)	Caucasian of Italian descent, Catholic	Girl, mother and father (veterinarians)	Older brother
Brazil (2)	Giovani (Boy)	Brazilian, Spiritualist	Boy and mother (salesperson)	Father (salesperson), older half brother
Brazil (3)	Maiara (Girl)	Brazilian, nonreligious	Girl and mother (salesperson)	Father (*capoeira*—Brazilian martial arts instructor)

Family musical background	Instruments and musical resources in the home	Child's participation in organized musical activities	Music in regular school?	Repertoires heard in the home
Parents never studied music formally	Digital player, CD, DVD	Recorder classes in school for two years, but not currently	No	*Sertanejo* (child's favorite), Brazilian popular music (MPB), soundtracks (*Os Incriveis*, a Mexican soap opera), *High School Musical*, *Shrek*, funk from Rio (sometimes)
Father never studied music formally, but is highly involved with community music (sings in choir, plays traditional Brazilian music)	*Abê*, *xequere*, *berimbau*, (Brazilian traditional instruments), keyboard, DVDs, CDs	Music classes in nursery school, but not currently	No	Alceu Valença (child's favorite), bossa-nova, MPB, Brazilian traditional music
Father never studied music formally, but learned traditional forms in the community, in his home state (i.e., Pernambuco); mother sang in a choir and took some guitar lessons as a child	Brazilian traditional instruments (shakers, *pandeiro*, *abê*), guitar, digital player	*Maracatu* (Brazilian folk musical practice) workshop, *capoeira* and percussion classes with parents	Child attends a strong music program offered by a local Waldorf school	"Feliz da Primavera" and "Sabiá"—children's tunes (child's favorites), Taiguara, Brazilian traditional music

(*continued*)

Table 0.3. *(continued)*

Country	Child (pseudonym and sex)	Ethnicity, nationality, cultural background, religion	Interviewees	Other family members (not interviewed)
Denmark	Catherine (Girl)	Danish	Girl and mother (self-employed graphic designer)	Father (self-employed chef), two brothers (one older, one younger)
Greece	Melina (Girl)	Greek, Orthodox	Girl and mother (dental technician)	Father (carpenter), older sister, older brother
Israel	Sissi (Girl)	Jewish	Girl and mother (music and movement therapist)	Two older sisters

Family musical background	Instruments and musical resources in the home	Child's participation in organized musical activities	Music in regular school?	Repertoires heard in the home
Mother played piano, recorder, and saxophone in her youth; brother is learning music	Keyboard, piano, nose flute, flute, computer with iTunes, stereo, microphones	Attended music classes for babies with mom between ages two and a half and five Began attending a choir at the Salvation Army at age five and continues with it	Yes	ABBA, classical music, Bob Dylan, Frank Zappa, Carla Bruni, Anne Linnet (Danish singer), Natasja Saad (one of child's favorite singers)
Not discussed	Guitar, electric piano, stereo, CDs	Latin dances (after-school program)	Yes, once a week (forty minutes)	Greek pop tunes by Michalis Chatziyiannis (child's favorite), children's tunes, classical music, Greek traditional music and byzantine chants
Mother is a professional musician. Everyone in the home seems to be involved in music; one sister plays the guitar	Cello, piano, recorder, guitar, world music instruments, flute, and others; mother collects musical instruments	Piano and cello lessons	Yes	Classical music, traditional Jewish tunes, songs from Disney's *The Little Mermaid* (in Hebrew)

(*continued*)

Table 0.3. (*continued*)

Country	Child (pseudonym and sex)	Ethnicity, nationality, cultural background, religion	Interviewees	Other family members (not interviewed)
Italy (1)	Federico (Boy)	Italian, Catholic	Boy, mother (nursery school teacher), father (electrician)	Older sister
Italy (2)	Anna (Girl)	Italian, Catholic	Girl and mother (clerk)	Father (clerk)
Kenya	Michael (Boy)	Gikuyu, Pentecostal Christian	Boy and father (logistics), mother joined at the end of interview (human resources)	Older sister
Netherlands (1)	Basje (Boy)		Boy, mother and father	

Family musical background	Instruments and musical resources in the home	Child's participation in organized musical activities	Music in regular school?	Repertoires heard in the home
Not informed	No instruments in the home; TV, CD, DVD, MP3, computer, radio, musical carpet "Karaballa," Nintendo, Wii	Not informed	Yes, once a week (one hour)	Tiziano Ferro (child's favorite) Lucio Dalla, Celine Dion, songs from Walt Disney and Pixar movies, *High School Musical*
Not informed	Computer musical games, Nintendo, TVs, computer, CD, DVD, stereo, child's own video camera	Music Together between ages four and five	Yes	Lady Gaga (child's favorite), Italian alphabet song, Spice Girls, Mariah Carey, Italian pop, *Madagascar* soundtrack, CD from the early childhood program *Music Together*
Father never studied music formally but loves music	Drums, keyboard, radio, TV, CD player	Piano lessons at school	Yes, once a week (forty minutes); instrumental lessons are offered for an extra fee	Not informed, but child sang a traditional children's song in English (i.e., "Mary Had a Little Lamb")
Mother sings in a choir; father defines himself as "not a music lover," but someone who enjoys music from time to time	Harmonica, piano	Scouts (current); music on the lap in infancy, had dance lessons at around ages four to five	Yes	Celine Dion (Child's favorite), Marillion, Doe Maar (Dutch), Coldplay, Anouk (Dutch), Ilse DeLang (Dutch)

(*continued*)

Table 0.3. (*continued*)

Country	Child (pseudonym and sex)	Ethnicity, nationality, cultural background, religion	Interviewees	Other family members (not interviewed)
Netherlands (2)	Rosa (Girl)		Girl, mother and father	
Singapore	Christine (Girl)	Chinese, Protestant	Girl, mother (homemaker), father (piano teacher)	
Spain	Maria (Girl)	Catalan, Catholic	Girl, mother (nurse)	Father (osteopath), younger sister, older sister
Taiwan	Annie (Girl)		Girl, mother (homemaker)	Father (financial analyst)
United Kingdom	Charlie (Girl)		Girl, father (not informed)	Older brother, mother (not informed)

Family musical background	Instruments and musical resources in the home	Child's participation in organized musical activities	Music in regular school?	Repertoires heard in the home
Mother took eight years of piano; father played piano and recorder in childhood	Piano, CDs	Music school (piano); musical theater at school	Yes	"I like the flowers"
Father is a piano teacher	Piano, CDs	Private voice lessons,	Occasionally	CD recordings of examination pieces from the Associated Board of the Royal Schools of Music and Trinity College of Music; musicals (*Annie*, *The Sound of Music*), classical music
Mom did not learn music growing up, but later learned how to play the guitar	*Djembe*, flute, plastic drum, Irish drum, didgeridoo, 2 flutes, recorder, guitar, boom box, CDs, computer	Guitar lessons with mother, twice a week; rhythmic gymnastics once a week (after school)	Yes, once a week (thirty minutes)	Jonas Brothers, Xesco Boix (Catalan singer), classical music, Miguel Bosé (favorite singer), Soundtrack to *Barbie, a Cinderella Story* (CD), Catalan stories with music
Mother was musically trained	Cello, piano (currently at grandparents' home)	Cello lessons, tap dancing, French, sports, cooking	Yes	Classical music, Yo Yo Ma, *Mamma mia!* (musical)
Older brother plays guitar; parents enjoy going out to pubs that have music	Violin, plastic drum, CDs, DVD, guitar, shakers, toy microphone, radio, iPod	Not discussed	Yes	"Robot parade" (child's favorite song), "They might be giants"

(*continued*)

Table 0.3. (*continued*)

Country	Child (pseudonym and sex)	Ethnicity, nationality, cultural background, religion	Interviewees	Other family members (not interviewed)
United States (1)	Brad (Boy)	Caucasian of East European descent, Protestant	Boy, father (attorney)	Younger sister, mother (homemaker)
United States (2)	Rose (Girl)	Caucasian of English and Polish descent, Protestant	Girl, mother (homemaker), father (realtor)	Older sister

playing major roles. That is, a strong interplay of local and global forces shape the musical parenting of seven-year-olds. Music educators need to be aware of these intricate influences and relationships, which have clear implications for practice in a wide range of educational settings.

Another important issue that remains elusive in music education is the role of social class in children's experiences. Although it is true that most of the research literature in music education has centered on middle-class children, it is also true that social class has usually served as an independent variable, in several earlier studies. Beatriz Ilari of the University of Southern California, USA, tackles this issue by considering the role of social class in children's (and families') home musical activities. She begins chapter 6 by emphasizing that all participating children came from the middle class, as locally articulated, and then she moves on to analyze three factors that have been commonly associated with middle-class parenting and families: autonomy and self-direction (Kohn, 1963), concerted cultivation (Lareau, 2011), and consumerism (Buckingham, 2011). Complement-

Family musical background	Instruments and musical resources in the home	Child's participation in organized musical activities	Music in regular school?	Repertoires heard in the home
Mom plays the piano; father likes music but never took any formal lessons	Piano, violin, electronic instruments, iPod, CDs, boom box, glockenspiel, hand drums, cymbals, toy trumpet, and toy piano	Piano and violin lessons; Kindermusik classes in early childhood	Yes, Kodály-based; frequency not informed	CDs of kids' rock and rap, classical music, children's music
Father is a singer; mother played the recorder	Parents' CDs, listening games on computer	Music classes in nursery school	Yes, Kodály-based; frequency not informed	"Somewhere over the Rainbow" (child's favorite song), country western, easy listening, 1970s music, children's music

ing Koutsoupidou's work (chapter 5), this chapter ends with a discussion of local and global issues surrounding middle-class musical childhoods.

The third section of the book is devoted to three chapters describing new developments or projects that emerged after the MyPlace, MyMusic data collection was completed. Two researchers were part of the original team (i.e., Lum and Persellin), and a third one (i.e., Woodward) joined the team later on.

In chapter 7, Diane Persellin of Trinity University, Texas, USA, discusses children's "open-earedness" to musical repertoires (Hargreaves, 1982). Three years after the data were collected, she revisited four children from the original study, to check whether their musical preferences and taste had changed. Her data revealed many changes in children's everyday listening experiences and preferences, which is consistent with past cross-sectional work and reports on potential changes in children's listening habits, as well as the pervasiveness of popular culture and music in the lives of tweens (see Bickford, 2011, 2012). Given the scarcity of longitudinal data on children's musical preferences and taste, Persellin's chapter raises many questions that are central to music education, including the degree of autonomy in children's musical choices, and whether musical taste is a product of child development, a social construction, or a combination of both.

In chapter 8, Sheila C. Woodward of Eastern Washington University, Cheney, Washington, USA, discusses the musical lives of two children in post-apartheid South Africa. Woodward joined the research team at a later time, and adapted the original research protocol to suit the needs of her participants. Her narrative approach offers readers a glimpse of her own experience growing up in South Africa during apartheid and how it relates to the musical experiences afforded to the children she interviewed. Woodward aligns with Tudge (2008) in her conclusion that the musical lives of the children interviewed in South Africa resonated with the musical lives of their parents. To some extent, this is also the conclusion of other chapters in the book (e.g., chapters 5, 6, and 10).

Chee-Hoo Lum of Nanyang Technological University, Singapore, is the author of chapter 10. A member of the original research team, Lum adapted the original MyPlace, MyMusic research protocol and used it as a learning tool in a music teacher education program. As a requirement of an elementary music methods class, sixteen Chinese preservice music teachers in Singapore were asked to interview one child and her/his parents following the MyPlace, MyMusic protocol, and then to submit a narrative to their instructor. Analyzing all sixteen narratives, Lum provides readers with much contextual information, including from the perspective of the Confucian ethos of music education. Lum's findings challenge universal notions of musical parenting, especially concerning musical values and repertoires, and, again, raising questions regarding the intricate relationships between the local and the global.

The book concludes with a discussion of the lessons learned from this complex research project, centering on two main areas. First, we describe what we have learned in relationship to qualitative inquiry. International collaboration, researcher and participant "situatedness," interview data, and ethics are some of the issues that are thoroughly discussed. Second, we examine the importance of the concept of musical childhood when studying children's engagement with music. We conclude the chapter by challenging notions of global child in music scholarship and music education in particular. Images of children, their homes, and musical instruments, as well as field notes and other data are also shared in the book. In keeping with the qualitative research tradition, readers may wish to turn to these sources as they read and reinterpret our analyses of data.[3]

Notes

1. Here we adopt the UNESCO definition of early childhood, which extends roughly from birth to age eight.

2. The entire research team was aware of this fact from the outset of the project.

3. Readers will also note that we have kept some terms in their original languages, including names of musical instruments and genres (see Table 0.3) and idiomatic expressions. Changing these terms would result in a misrepresentation of their meanings because some do not translate well into English. Examples include *abê* (a type of Brazilian drum), and the Malay term *atas* for high class (in Singapore).

SECTION I

Theoretical Framework and Methods

1 Musical Childhoods

Theoretical Background and New Directions

Susan Young

In undertaking this project we aimed not only to increase our knowledge of children's everyday and home-based musical experiences but also to contribute to a shift in the theoretical paradigm within which children are being conceptualized musically. In recent years there has been a noticeable change in the way that children's musical activities and experiences are being viewed and understood. A number of texts have focussed on children's musical cultures in a range of locations (e.g., Boynton and Kok, 2006; Campbell and Wiggins, 2014; Whiteman and Lum, 2012). These recent texts were motivated by a new recognition that children have their own musical cultures and have mastery over them. They were also motivated by a recognition that hitherto the scope and force of children's musical cultures had been unappreciated. The approach is primarily ethnomusicological with a focus on the music made by children in relation to cultural context. So, broadly speaking, our project joins a body of recent work that is moving in similar directions. Here, however, we propose a theoretical position for framing our work that draws on the field of Childhood Studies as it has been developed in the UK and Scandinavia. In this respect our theoretical position is distinctive in some aspects. Sometimes known as the "new" (although now not so "new") social studies of childhood (see, e.g., James, Jenks, and Prout, 1998), Childhood Studies (the UK/Scandinavian version) is a generic term for a theoretical approach that is cross-disciplinary but firmly rooted in contemporary sociology and anthropology of childhood (Kehily, 2008). Having originated in the later 1990s, this field is now "coming of age" and many of the theoretical positions are well worked and debated. Development of a notion of musical childhoods from a Childhood Studies perspective offers, we propose, a theoretical framework that can provide useful and illuminating viewpoints from which to explore and discuss children's musical experiences and activities.

Because a notion of musical childhoods rooted in Childhood Studies represents a departure from the usual ways that music in childhood has been theorized, I start this chapter by explaining conventional approaches and some of their potential shortcomings. Psychology is the primary lens through which children's experiences in music have been, and continue to be, researched and interpreted. Approaches rooted in developmental psychology have been concerned with identifying pathways of musical progress through ages and stages. Psychology as a frame for understanding childhood has been criticized from a number of perspectives. One major criticism is that it purports to arrive at homogeneous versions of children's (musical) activity that are assumed to apply to all children, universally. In its focus on finding the commonalities in children's musical activity, psychology has been less interested in identifying variations and differences. This focus results in neglect of the social and cultural contexts and how these might be intrinsically bound up with children's musical experience and learning. Psychology has been a powerful voice in music education theory and practice, defining what musical childhood is and how it can be understood.

In contrast to psychology, sociology has sought to understand how children are socialized into society and learn to become members of the social groups in which they live. Sociologically oriented work in the field of children's music that explores processes of enculturation and socialization into traditions of music may be less prominent than psychologically oriented work (and certainly less influential on education theory and practice), but there are some examples of work in which socialization is assumed. Many of these examples overlap with anthropology and ethnomusicology, and also with popular music studies, where research into children's music is mainly interested in how children and young people are apprenticed into cultural traditions. The process of socialization in these accounts generally assumes that children are fairly passive and that they simply absorb the music around them, rather than actively appropriating and in the process, transforming. A set of chapters edited by Boynton and Kok (2006), for example, describe and discuss how children are socialized into the musical worlds of their communities: historical, traditional, and present-day.

Conceptions of children as musical in theories concerned with "development" and "socialization" are interested in children's music making for how it can be related to adult music making as the final achievement. And all too often the adult "endpoints" are assumed and these, in turn, are drawn selectively from conventional adult practices of Western art music. For example, children's instrumental improvisations have been analyzed for evidence of rhythmic and melodic structures that conform to formal conventions and not analyzed with a view to understanding children's own, more intuitive ways of thinking musically. Similarly, singing development has been assumed to proceed through a set of stages before children reach the full capacity to sing as adults, and researchers have debated, as many still do, the details of sequential steps. Researchers have been less interested in children's songs and how singing is a personally and socially meaningful activity for children in their own worlds of peers and family. As many have succinctly put it, the focus has been on children's "becoming" and not on their "being." Models of socialization, although less prevalent in music, were also criticized for assuming that children were passively shaped by processes and practices in the family and wider community.

Childhood Studies staked out its ground by critiquing these dominant approaches to conceptualizing children and by opposing the tendencies to view children as passive rather than active, irrational rather than rational, and incompetent versus competent—in other words, as in some ways incomplete and lacking. Instead, early childhood studies scholars such as James, Jenks, and Prout (1998) called for theoretical premises and research methods that could reveal the ways in which children demonstrate competence—and on their own terms, not those predetermined by theories that assumed adult competences (and as Burman [1994], has pointed out not just adult, but Western, white, and male) to be the final destination of development or socialization. As childhood studies has become more established, the initial, strongly opposing stance adopted in the early days has itself been recognized as problematic, as somewhat rigid and uncompromising, and containing some inherent weaknesses (e.g., Woodhead, 1999). More recently scholars have looked for more reconciliatory positions that can incorporate "both/and" positions.

Meanwhile social anthropology and sociology also woke up to the fact that both fields had marginalized children in much the same way that they had marginalized women and other subordinate social groups. Just as women's studies sought to give voice, agency, and identity to women, so the "new" social studies of childhood, influenced by feminist arguments and methods, sought to give voice, agency, and identity to children. Anthropology's important contribution was to explore childhoods in varying locations and contexts, and thereby to draw attention to the diversity of children's lives and the diversity of ideas about childhood (Tudge, 2008). Although anthropology had traditionally studied the cultures of "others" living in far-off places, in recent years, it has moved closer to home (although "home" continues to be the developed world for most anthropologists) and has adapted its methods of ethnography, participant observation, and thick description to study everyday life among social groups in the developed world, including children. An excellent example is the work of Lareau (2011), which is based on ethnographies of children living in varying social circumstances in the United States. Importantly, social anthropology seeks to arrive at understandings based on the perspectives of those it studies rather than study responses to predetermined categories of behavior. Researchers working in the field have sought to introduce methodological innovations that enable children to be the subjects rather than the objects of research and to work with children in more participatory ways that enable them to voice their views. From these methodological innovations, versions of childhood experience emerged that started to give a very different picture of children's daily lives and experiences. In music fields we see these changes filtering through into ethnomusicology and historical musicology, resulting in the upsurge of activity in studying children's musical cultures in recent years.

Thus from a number of disciplinary directions, the ways in which childhood was viewed and researched began to change fundamentally and these changes began to coalesce within the field of Childhood Studies (see Young, 2009, 2012a). A key theoretical contribution of Childhood Studies, using poststructuralist theoretical arguments, has been to demonstrate how circulating discourses create common meanings or "constructions" of childhood (Fleer, Hedegard, and Tudge, 2008; James and Prout, 1997). From this standpoint it becomes evident that there are many different constructions of childhood (and here we consider musical childhoods), and that these different versions are a product of social and cultural processes that vary across time and place. Children are seen not as formed by natural, biological, or psychological processes or by social forces, but as inhabiting a world of meaning created through their interactions with the material and social properties available within their surrounding milieu, or worlds. In this chapter we identify and then discuss these worlds as corporate/consumer, peer, parent and family, education, and community. These are five dominant areas that emerge from our work. Adopting this viewpoint, psychological accounts of childhood are seen as just one form of sociocultural construction alongside many others and not the neutral, natural, scientifically validated, and universal model they are assumed to be. Likewise one can go on to discern and formulate the kinds of musical childhoods held, for example, in the ideologies of parents who negotiate their aspirations for their children with a number of competing pressures. Or one can identify the constructions of musical childhoods held in the marketing strategies of large corporations seeking to maximize profits from the sale of commodity musical items for children.

Importantly, a view that understands childhood as socially constructed provides not only a framework for identifying different modes of musical childhood but also a technique for considering how and why childhood is constructed in these ways. It then becomes apparent that the different musical childhoods blend with, compete with, or reinforce one another, and that children negotiate their own way through them. We asked the children, for example, to choose their favorite song to sing to us. The children knew that their selection of a song was not a neutral process. The song they chose would signal certain allegiances, associations, and values and would signal these within that momentary situation of a researcher's asking—with or without parents present—for "your favorite song." If they chose a school song this might signal conformity that would bring approval from parents, but maybe not the pleasures of allegiance to a peer group that singing a popular song might bring. Thus childhood studies also provides a critical framework that can highlight how musical childhoods operate within competing demands and reveal the subtle pressures for conformity and rewards for compliance.

One of the potential problems with a view of childhood as culturally constructed, however, is that it can suggest that different forms of childhood are imposed on children. It can imply a passive process of inculcation and molding by social forces rather than an active process of appropriation. Musical childhoods, accordingly, are not a predetermined set of categories, but something that children engage in and are actively involved in shaping. In this sense children are understood to engage in processes of co-construction, to be actively choosing the favorite song they sing with awareness of its wider meanings. This is a sociocultural conception of development that differs markedly from the conceptions of development held in psychology and sociology. Childhood Studies theory focuses on agency and seeks to describe the agentive and co-constructed nature of experiences for children. However, it has to be recognized that agency operates within the constraints and possibilities offered by sociocultural contexts. This means that children are always in some way constrained by the historical and culturally defined discourses that invest them, their bodies, and actions, with certain meanings. Children may be agentive, but in some accounts of children as musical, particularly in a progressive educational vein, there is a strong desire to see them as highly agentive in an idealized way that tends to overlook the realities, the constraints, and limitations on their agency. The idealistically competent child, the savvy so-called digital native, for example, is a sociocultural construction born of a particular viewpoint. One only needs to bring into the picture children living in disadvantaged circumstances—take the extreme example of street children living in developing world cities—and it becomes clear that the capacity to exercise agency for the majority of the world's children is limited by poverty, ill-health, disability, conflict, inadequate housing, work and care commitments, lack of support structures, and so on. Therefore, agency as a theoretical concept for understanding children's musical childhoods is useful only if it is accompanied by a full and detailed consideration of the possibilities for agency offered by the surrounding sociocultural context. Without this situational detail, agency can easily fall back into essentialist notions of children and elide with romantic ideas of children as occupying special worlds that are separate from those of adults. Children's worlds are never separate. On the contrary, the surrounding society offers certain niches within which children can exert their agency, and gaining an understanding of the affordances offered by those niches becomes a key task—hence our interest in understanding the home as a "niche" for children's musical activity.

So there is also a need to consider carefully how the context, the niche, or culture, whatever terminological slant is adopted, is defined. Accounts of musical experiences for children in diverse social and historical contexts can tend to assume self-contained cultural contexts and traditions of music that are static and unchanging (see, for example, some chapters in Boynton and Kok, 2006). This assumption often goes hand in hand with a musicological standpoint that starts by foregrounding the musical genre or musical performance occasion representative of certain musical cultures. The participants then become secondary. For example, take the interest in children's playground and singing games in which the initial focus has been on documenting the songs and games as musical objects, and then the children's forms of participation are integrated into that primary focus (e.g., Opie and Opie, 1988). Likewise in some recent accounts of children's musical cultures, describing the "culture" comes first. In our project we start in reverse, with individual children, and we are interested in how they are shaping their own musical lives. This means that our focus is their everyday activities and the breadth of that activity networked across their lives and the lives of others. We are interested in what to some other researchers may appear to be trivial and commonplace, and therefore unworthy of serious attention: their toys, their musical items, their bedroom play activities, music equipment in the communal family living spaces, what music they hear day-to-day at home, and so on. We are also interested in how their musical activities intersect with their social relationships, both with family and with peers and other adults beyond the home (although in this study our focus was the family and any information about peers or other adults was secondary) and how they use the people and things in their daily lives to create these musical experiences. We also, notably, start with asking the children about their everyday musical experiences and then inquire outward, leading on to questions about community and school music.

We centered the children in their homes and also asked about wider contexts of school and community, but we should stress that we do not hold a spatial view of ever-widening circles of activity as in Bronfenbrenner's (1979) ecological systems theory. We notice that Bronfenbrenner's theory has been adopted in some recent explanations of children's musical activity (Whiteman, 2014). This theoretical concept, for us, collapses with the rapid increase of domestic digital technologies. The peripheral cultural worlds of music now enter directly into the home via technologies that can beam and download digital music and music in multimodal media form from the outer reaches of Bronfenbrenner's notion of expanding cultural domains. So for us, the notion of expanding distance implied in Bronfenbrenner's theory no longer exist; at least, not in the same clear-cut structure. As Ito et al. (2009) have also asserted, since the advent of television and more so with the advent of the internet children are getting "out" more, into the virtual spaces produced through media networks, both real and imaginary. And likewise the real and imaginary spaces of children's media are also moving "in" more to the musical subjectivities of children, and integrating with domestic "micropolitics" as Ito and colleagues term it. Moreover, as they emphasize, this process is linked to and motivated by a large and growing industry.

So to return to the argument that "culture" is all too often left under-theorised in discussions of children's music and a concept of "culture" that is concrete, static and self-contained tends to be assumed. Such a concept of culture then leads to ideas such as border crossing: assumptions that somehow children travel between these fixed and preexisting "cultures" of music or musical worlds and rework music on their own terms as they go. Anthropology, the discipline that studies cultures in their diversity, has become increasingly wary of the concept of culture, recognizing how problematic it is. At the same time, interestingly, it has become a more active concept in other disciplinary fields. Education, for example, has reshaped educational theory to be more sensitive to social and cultural context. Anthropology, meanwhile, increasingly emphasizes the dynamic, shifting, and fluid nature of cultures, particularly with the increase in the global movement and communication between populations. Recent scholarship has recast culture as performative, that is, as a set of practices that are continually emergent and forming. A concept of culture as practice, as an emergent process rather than fixed and static, can encompass the interaction between capacities for agency that individual children possess and the opportunities for agency allowed for by the context—the material and social structure.

At this point in the discussion it is useful to remind readers that in relation to the movement of populations, one of our criteria for selection of the children in this project was to select a child who belonged to the same ethnicity and lived in the same locality as the researcher (i.e., a child who had not migrated to the locality). Our primary reason for this stipulation was methodological. We assumed that researchers would draw from their circle of friends and family to find "their child" and we also thought that similarity of language and ethnicity would help to smooth the research relationships. We also knew that the transcultural processes of migration were likely to complicate our formulation of musical childhoods. However we *are* aware that any contemporary theory needs to recognize the increasingly mobile transcultural processes that are incorporated into musical childhoods. Marsh (2009), for example, in her studies of immigration and children's music, has contributed much to our understanding of transcultural musical childhoods. Children who have migrated, or whose parents migrated before them, often have home musical experiences that do not derive from one particular place or country but are changing and absorbing from multiple sources.

We thus propose that theoretically the notion of musical childhoods as constructed offers a useful template for theorizing and understanding the musical niches in any given society within which children can exercise their agency. Theoretically we emphasize the inseparable duality, or dialectic, of agency and structure/environmental possibilities, between actual practice and systems of meaning. In this project we use this theoretical perspective as a template for helping us to make sense of the children's domestic musical activities, although we propose that it could be widely adopted in other contexts. It is, however, a template, and in that sense offers a broad, orienting theoretical framework but little more. Due to its breadth, it can also incorporate the psychological and educational conceptions of children's musical growth and learning. It can incorporate the conceptions of children's participation in musical cultures via the media, or local musical cultures. It can incorporate all the illuminating forms of musical childhood that cultural, sociological, and ethnomusicological studies are revealing. By bringing these hitherto separate versions under one theoretical template, they can be set side by side and questions can be asked. We can examine how musical childhoods are modeled, reproduced, managed, reinforced, and resourced.

However, as Rose (1999) has emphasized, it is not enough to suggest that childhood is socially constructed because this is something of a theoretical dead-end. Instead one must go on to explore and explain *how* childhood is constructed in particular contexts. He suggests that we need to ask, "which authorities are able to pronounce upon them and through what concepts and explanatory regimes are they specified?"(Rose, 1999, pp. x–xi). The following sections propose different "worlds" or niches and how they act as "authorities" that define versions of musical childhoods, which then offer to children a range of affordances or possibilities for action. What also becomes informative is where the different worlds may be congruent and affirm and reinforce one another, or where they may be in conflict and tension. We found many small examples of how the worlds of peer and popular culture might converge but, there again, diverge from the worlds of parents and teachers. The critical theory perspective within childhood studies also calls for identification of the power structures that operate in articulating the potentials and constraints within these versions of musical childhood and thereby serve to advantage some children and disadvantage others. I return to this point after a discussion of the different worlds of musical childhood to which I now turn.

The Corporate/Consumer World

Many have discussed the commercialization of childhood from a range of perspectives (for an overview, see Pugh, 2009). The corporate world has redefined musical childhoods according to marketing criteria by which the maximizing of profit takes precedence over any other educational or public service aims. Our project revealed the range of commercial musical items made available to children in their homes (see Ilari, chapter 6, this volume). By the term *items* we have in mind both the material equipment (toys, instruments, books and magazines, technology equipment) and the digital media they enable (music, video games, films, TV programs). As Ito and colleagues (2009) emphasize, the assumption of passive consumption of media items such as television may be challenged by contemporary popular culture, which provides more opportunities for the active exercise of agency via technologized music-play activities. For Charlie, a UK girl, a new gift of a Bratz video game linked virtual dolls with her real doll, and it would thus be one small step farther to access Bratz Kidz websites that also link with social media.

The material and media items are increasingly intertextual, meaning that content is linked and cross-referenced across a media mix of television, books, magazines, toys, film, internet sites, video games, everyday household items such as clothing, bedding, food utensils and packaging, even the food itself. The corporate musical culture for younger children may be congruent with the parents' image of young musical childhoods. Charlie in the UK is proud to show the musical puppet she has had since babyhood that plays a nursery rhyme tune. But as children age, "kinderculture," as Steinberg and Kincheloe (1997) term it, starts to run parallel with the adult world of educators and parents. Giovanna in Brazil is proud to sing two of her favorite songs: the theme to the children's film *Shrek* and the romantic country music ballad by *sertanejo* artists Victor and Leo, both of which she will have learned from commercial media sources accessed at home. But as children enter middle childhood, or the tween years, the corporate media system and musical merchandise may arouse anxiety and concern among parents who then seek to manage, possibly restricting, their children's access to such items. The mother of Annie in Taiwan directly expressed her concerns about her daughter's viewing of a film she thought unsuitable for her age and her attempts to control her daughter's access to such items. As children age, there may be concerns about their growing up too quickly and too soon, or that the commodified musical items carry class, racial, and sexualized connotations. Some parents expressed concerns about premature sexualization of children, particularly through pop-song lyrics. Our seven-year-olds were on the brink of accessing contemporary popular culture with more independence, and with that comes the risk (in the parents' eyes) of bypassing their parents and other adults such as teachers.

There is another interesting strand of music as commodity in the form of music classes for children and instrumental lessons that are private, fee paying, and take place outside of mainstream school hours. This may even extend to the system of music examinations, most notably the system run by the Associated Board of the Royal Schools of Music. This strand merges with the parental and educational worlds in that it may affirm many of the same values and images of what constitutes a "good" musical childhood. In some parts of the world, particularly the Far East, for children to progress in playing Western art music according to the examination system is thought to bestow many benefits in the child's preparation for future life as Lum (chapter 9, this volume) explains. For the UK father, however, formal music lessons challenged some of his values for he prioritized freedom from pressure and self-initiated and creative play for his daughter.

The Peer World

Children's encounters with peers occur at school and opportunities to play with friends at home and in public spaces. The peer culture, concerned with "longing and belonging" (Pugh, 2009), merges with the corporate. The corporate world, driven by profit motives, looks for ways to create desire for its products and thereby to increase sales. Increasing desirability by associating certain media items with belonging and identification with peer cultures is one market ploy. Thus fads and fashions are cultivated that act as markers of belonging. Others have written about the tween music worlds that are appealing to children just entering middle childhood because they beckon a world they aspire to—a world of "growing up" (Bickford, 2012). Our children at home were participating in musical activities without direct peer contact, but the presence of peers was felt vicariously through the types of activities that the children considered to be age appropriate and to have status.

Parent and Family World

As Jenks (1996) points out, changes in the way children are seen reflect broader adult concerns about identity and security in changing times. In what is known as the "risk" culture, parents seek to mobilize what means they have to prepare children for their future, but at the same time, parents seek to protect their children from what they perceive as dangers and pressures.

The parents constructed children's musical worlds as a "time and place apart" both literally, in the sense of items to support time spent alone at home, often in bedroom spaces, and metaphorically, in creating children's musical worlds replete with symbolic meaning. For some this meaning was of innocence, happiness, and lack of responsibilities, for others it was about protection and enclosure in the family and about reinforcing commitments and identity along ethnic and religious lines. Several of the children lived in families affluent enough to provide them with single bedrooms for their sole use. Charlie in the UK had a bedroom that was full of her own toys and included a radio that she could listen to. But the radio's linkage to any number of radio stations was problematic for her and she asked her father to tune it, and set it on one pop-music station that she preferred. The spoken news programs, in particular, troubled her. Thus she imposed some of her own limitations and did not rely only on her parents to structure her childhood activities. On a shelf in the bedroom was the aforementioned Bratz doll, with long blond hair, dressed in pop-star clothing with a short skirt. Alongside the doll was the Bratz tour bus, part of a play scenario that included the Bratz girl band on tour. At the same time, she showed me small toy drums from her bath time and a tinkling music box. At this age her musical world in the family seemed to consist of an easy blend of an early childhood world of toys, closely tied in to self-initiated play, with the first inroads into a tween-age world of dolls representing adult lifestyles and celebrity, pop-music worlds.

At the same time, several parents held aspirations for formally framed "academic" and career achievements in the musical futures of their children. Chee Hoo Lum (chapter 9) discusses in detail the future-oriented aspirations that middle-class Singaporean parents of Chinese descent held for the children. Other children in the project had formal cello and piano lessons, choir singing outside of school, and dance certificates. We noticed that some parents interpreted the research visit and home video occasion as an opportunity to display their children's musical achievements, thus revealing their dominant image of a "musical" childhood and what they most valued. Annie, the Taiwanese girl, for example, performed pieces from her instrumental repertoire, perhaps reflecting the parents' perceptions of the purpose of the study and their association of childhood with academic achievements.

The method of home visits via video recordings and including interviews with parents captured the parents' ideas about music for their children. Two parents, for example, subtly censored what the children showed. The Greek mother tried to suppress her daughter's wish to sing a football song as her "favorite song" in preference to a more acceptable (in her eyes) school song. When Basje, the Dutch boy showed and talked about the CDs he possessed at home, or family CDs that he liked to listen to, his mother took one CD from him that presented a female singer in sexualized pose on the cover and seemed to be of two minds about his showing it. The moment seemed to encapsulate the tension for parents who want to give their children free choice and yet, at the same time, become uneasy if they perceive that their children are engaging in activities that do not represent and affirm an image of childhood that they hold, particularly in relation to premature sexuality. The English father talked of wanting his daughter to enjoy music and not to find it a chore—a dilemma that explained his delay in arranging violin lessons, which he perceived as chore-like. Thus we understood "our" parents to be constantly monitoring their children's activities, making many small adjustments, and attempting to guide them to conform to their own ideas of what makes a "good childhood," and to their own identity aspirations related to class and ethnicity.

Unsurprisingly, children's musical preferences were also highly influenced by their parents' musical worlds. Charlie's favorite CD was one recorded by her father's own amateur pop group. We learn from several of the children how they learned particular "adult" repertoires from their parents' own preferences and CD collections. Far from being neutral (Green, 1997), these repertoires were directly linked to parental interests, values, and belief systems. Interestingly, in several instances the fathers' musical collections influenced the children's musical choices. This perhaps reflects the fact that, typically, it is often men who collect and possess CD collections.

Education Worlds

Educators define musical childhoods according to educational criteria, defined by expert, psychology-influenced versions of musical childhood that, as already explained, are oriented to the progressive learning of skills associated, almost exclusively, with Western art music. The education version may also be congruent with parental aspirations for academic achievement, but less congruent with corporate and peer versions. Thus the different constructions of childhood may conflict or coincide. The education world seeped into the home environment to different degrees in the different children's worlds. The request to "sing their favorite song" often resulted in their offering a song from school. Song singing remains a dominant activity in educational music activity, particularly in this age phase, and it is thus understandable that this element of the educational world would most readily permeate the home environment. Aside from the song singing, and the influence of instrumental lessons on those who received them, the education world appeared to be a very small component of the overall musical worlds of the children. When asked about school music, Charlie offered some brief descriptions of activities from school, but seemed little interested in pursuing this topic and quickly returned to discuss her father's pop group CD. I took this as an indication of the music that was most meaningful to her. Viewed from the child's position within their home, the influence of education worlds seemed a small and fairly minor part in terms of meaningfulness to many of the children. Viewed from the educators' position, educational music is perhaps assumed to carry more significance to children than is the case in reality. For the children in our study, the influence of media music worlds and their family and community music worlds seemed to be far greater.

Community Worlds

The local community, particularly in the form of religious institutions, sport, or leisure activities, may offer additional modes of musical participation that "construct" alternative versions of musical childhood. Some children attended church or temple services and participated in music for worship. Lum (this volume) describes the way that the children's accomplishments in instrumental playing might then integrate with their participation in church or temple. Participation in church services might offer musical experiences that the children draw on in constructing their identities. For example, Michael, from Kenya, discovered drums at church. For some families, community musical events such as street dancing, provided an opportunity to participate in musical experiences that carried strong connotations of national identity. The parents steer their children to be musical in ways that conform to their own valued religious and national musical experiences. At the age of seven none of our children were attending musical occasions in the local community, which the parents did not actively manage and therefore sanction. Typically, contemporary children in the developed world—especially those living in urban areas—have very little freedom outside of their homes to participate of their own volition in community music events.

Conclusions

Although we have teased apart different articulations of musical childhood in order to explore and discuss how they are constructed, it is important to stress that they are operating in concert, not separately. The notion of moving along a developmental pathway to a fixed and certain endpoint is replaced by this more fluid, emergent process of interaction between the generative potentials possessed by the child—agency, in other words—and the potentials, the affordances, offered by the environment. Deleuze and Guattari's (1987) metaphor of the rhizome to replace the linear treelike model (rooted and growing upward) usefully encapsulates how the process is heterogeneous and multiple. A rhizome can be entered from many different points, all of which connect to each other. The rhizome does not have a beginning, an end, or an exact center. Although there are shifting hierarchies, or operations of power and influence, between the different modes of musical childhood, no one mode has the monopoly on defining and representing musical childhood. They operate together in reciprocal ways.

Finally, what is also valuable about a view from Childhood Studies is that it can be destabilizing. Behind Childhood Studies is a strong ethical mission to point out injustices toward children and argue for their redress. This is particularly so where power and privilege can result in uneven and unfair opportunities for some children at the expense of others. How, for example, do the universalizing constructs of children within psychology subtly underscore some models of musicality and result in sets of norms according to which children are rigidly educated and assessed (Rose, 1999, p. 154)? How do the commodified versions of musical childhood channel children into rigid gender-differentiated roles, or reinforce stereotypes of race and class so that children's opportunities for agency are restricted? We might equally inquire whether some corporate images of musical childhoods carry the risks many fear, and study carefully the way that children actively use media in their own ways before jumping to hasty conclusions.

We might ask whether different parenting styles lead to variations in musical childhoods that privilege some children and disadvantage others and whether interventions can remedy that situation.

How we think about and define musical childhoods matters very much because our views, ideas, and theories affect how our societies—schools, parents, community settings, arts organizations, corporations, music and media companies—engage with children in their everyday lives and practice. Finally, if the role of education is to maximize opportunities for children and attempt to redress any disadvantages—for all of us undertaking this project are educators by profession and at heart—then understanding constructions of musical childhoods, particularly in their contemporary forms, is a necessary preliminary stage in the design of educational interventions.

2 The Project Wiki

Enabling and Transforming the Methods and Processes of Research

Jèssica Pérez-Moreno

In this chapter, I describe and discuss the adoption of a wiki platform to support the processes of collaborative research carried out by the team participating in the international project MyPlace, MyMusic. The aim of the chapter is twofold: on the one hand, it highlights how the adoption of the wiki enabled and transformed the research methods and processes and, on the other hand, it also hopes to encourage other research teams to adopt a social media platform as a framework for gathering data for their studies.

This chapter is composed of six sections. First, I present an overview of how technology can be highly efficient in research collaborations. Here the concepts of Web 2.0 social computing and social media are introduced to give the reader a wider perspective. In the next section, I summarize the aspects of the MyPlace, MyMusic project that are pertinent to this chapter and follow with a description of the technical processes involved in the adoption of a wiki. Subsequently, I consider knowledge creation through collaborative innovation, the approach that the wiki has spotlighted for the participants. Later, I review issues that emerged during the course of the wiki project and that deserve further study. Finally, I conclude by identifying how the adoption of a wiki strengthened collaborative research work among the participating team.

Overview: Benefits of Technologically Mediated Collaboration in Research

Over the past few years, advances in technology have generated changes in both how we live and how we work. Computers have become a mainstay at home, propagated by their affordability and the associated support services as well as by the development of broadband and wireless connectivity. We can access the World Wide Web from virtually anywhere now.

In the new millennium, the development of Web 2.0 tools changed our relationship with the internet. These new tools facilitated the creation, development, and sharing of collective intelligence using innovative platforms. We moved from being an audience of passive consumers of content, to being participants, taking an active role in the construction of content—that is, we became contributors. At the same time, we moved from individual interaction to participation with others, emphasizing the social potential of the web. As stated by Parameswaran and Whinston (2007a, p. 769), "the networked environment is now closer to the user, and the users are empowered for personal expression and communal interaction."

Due to the importance of the social mass in Web 2.0 technologies, a series of interactive platforms grouped under the name of social media were developed. Kaplan and Haenlein (2010, p. 61) define social media as "a group of internet-based applications that build on the ideological and technological foundations of Web 2.0 and that allow the creation and exchange of user-generated content." This new form of media, which fosters human communication, shares most or all of the following characteristics (Mayfield, 2008):

- *Participation*: levels are so high that the dividing line between media and audience becomes blurred. The approach is bottom-up instead of top-down.
- *Openness*: there are no restrictions. Everyone is welcome to lurk and post. There is an active community regulating each site.
- *Conversation versus broadcasting*: in Web 2.0 the conversations are two-way.
- *Community*: the power of the social media lies in the fact that they enable communities to initiate and maintain effective communication with and among their members.
- *Connectedness*: the dynamic content of social media allows for the constant addition of links to sites, resources and people.

Social computing is another term used to refer to internet-based software that facilitates communication, information sharing, and open collaboration. It is an area of computer science that studies the intersection of social behavior and computational systems (*Social Computing*, 2012). Social computing has developed widely over the past twenty years, thanks to the rapid rise in the use of social media. One of the claims of social computing is that social media have an influence on and reflect the wider processes of society (Parameswaran and Whinston, 2007a, 2007b).

The principles of social computing can be applied through social media platforms. Kaplan and Haenlein (2010) classify social media platforms using a six-point scheme. Each of them provides insight into the study of virtual human interaction:

- *Collaborative projects*: these permit simultaneous, multifaceted creation of content. It is probably the most democratic manifestation of the social media, where "the joint effort of many actors leads to a better outcome than

what any actor could achieve individually" (Kaplan and Haenlein, 2010, p. 62). Wikis and social bookmarking tools are examples of this approach, with Wikipedia probably being the most famous of all collaborative projects.
- *Blogs and microblogs*: these are the oldest form of social media. This kind of communication, one (author) to many (readers) reminds us of how personal websites used to work; now, readers can post via a predesigned platform. Twitter is currently the most popular application of this kind.
- *Content communities*: these allow users to share content of specific multimedia materials (photos, texts, videos, music, and so on). Over the past few years YouTube has been at the forefront of this form of social media.
- *Social networking sites*: these platforms allow users to display and share personal information. Facebook is one of the best examples.
- *Virtual game worlds and virtual social worlds*: virtual realities where users participate and interact with one another in imaginary worlds.

In summary, the following lines from Mayfield (2008, p. 7) express the success of social media phenomena very aptly:

> A good way to think about social media is that all of this is actually just about being human beings. Sharing ideas, cooperating and collaborating to create art, thinking and commerce, vigorous debate and discourse, finding people who might be good friends, allies and lovers—it's what our species has built several civilisations on. That's why it is spreading so quickly, not because it's great shiny, whizzy new technology, but because it lets us be ourselves—only more so.

As mentioned earlier, social computing offers new opportunities and potentials for research, in particular by providing geographically dispersed participants with communication platforms (Castaños and Piercy, 2010; Young and Pérez, 2012), and by allowing the management of multimodal data. Both of these potentials were fundamental to this study.

The MyPlace, MyMusic Project

The foundations of the MyPlace, MyMusic project were laid out during the International Society for Music Education Commission for Early Childhood 2008 Seminar. A group of researchers met face-to-face to establish the general guidelines of the project, the goal of which was to increase our understanding of home-based musical experiences among young children (Young et al., 2010). As discussed in the introduction, a common protocol was drawn up and then sent to the participating researchers, a diverse team of scholars from all over the world. The goal of the MyPlace, MyMusic project was to identify themes and patterns that emerged through an inductive process of interpreting data collected at various international locations.

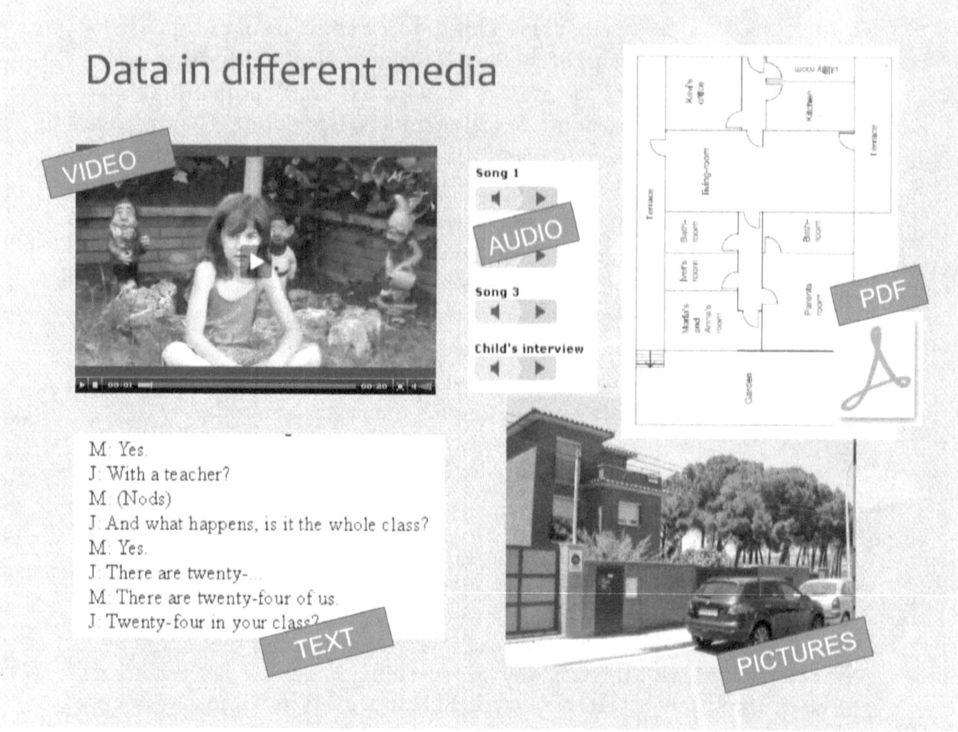

Figure 2.1. Multiple sources of data for the Wiki. Picture of Spanish child published with parental permission.

To capture the reality of the seven-year-old interviewees we employed a variety of methods that are specified in the protocol and explained in detail in the introduction.[1] Furthermore, the data collected also had to be diverse and multimodal in nature and included photographs, texts, video and audio recordings, as well as some PDF files (see Figure 2.1). After the home visits each participant sent his or her files to the project coordinator, who was responsible for sorting out and organizing the information. Envelopes containing CDs and/or DVDs started to arrive. Soon two main questions occupied our attention:

- How do we organize the data and how do we manage it so that each researcher can easily access the data of other researchers?
- What can we do to keep the project open to new countries?

Bearing in mind that the community of participating researchers was self-funded and the collected data multimodal, it was necessary to devise an efficient, low-cost strategy that would be viable and useful in the long run. At the time, we believed that a social media format would be optimal because it offered all the features of complex and expensive information technology solutions at no charge (Sauer et al., 2005).

Establishing the Wiki

As noted, we were aware that the characteristics of the collected data and the research community entailed a technical, effective, low-cost solution as a means of returning information to each contributor. After considering different platforms we decided to use a wiki, a social media form designed in 1995 by Ward Cunningham to facilitate collaborative content authoring, information sharing, and knowledge creation (Gears, 2011). The wiki was defined by its creator as "a freely expandable collection of interlinked Web pages, a hypertext system for storing and modifying information—a database, where each page is easily edited by any user with a forms-capable Web browser client" (Leuf and Cunningham, 2001, p. 14).

After a thorough literature search we were unable to find any research on music education that discussed the process of setting up a wiki or, indeed, even used one (Young and Pérez, 2012). Now the most common topics in relation to wikis focus on interactions in learning communities (e.g., Kim, Miller, Herbert, Pedersen, and Loving, 2012; Wheeler, Yeomans, and Wheeler, 2008), the development of Wikipedia (e.g., Baytiyeh and Pfaffman, 2009; Eijkman, 2010; Ozturk, 2012), and the implementation of social media formats, wikis specifically, in business environments (e.g., Gears, 2011; Milovanovic, Minovic, Stavljanin, Savkovic, and Starcevic, 2012).

As Gears (2011, p. 12) points out, it is well known that "wikis provide low-cost means for collaborative content development, and emergence of knowledge enabled in a repository of collective intelligence." Several features of wikis made them a very suitable resource for our community and the purposes of the study. A wiki has the following advantages:

- It is a *free social media resource*, which makes it affordable for a self-funding community.
- It features a *real-time database*, which implies that everybody, regardless of their location, can see the contributions at the same time they were made. It is interesting to note that "wiki" is a Hawaiian word meaning "quick," implying this is its key characteristic.
- It offers *easy access everywhere*. Having an internet connection is the only requirement.
- It permits *shared treatment of the data*. Every member of the research team can upload and edit the data, which fosters independence since one does not need to ask permission to contribute nor the help of an expert to do it.

- *It serves to build multimodal data banks.* Different kinds of media (texts, pictures, videos, and so on) can be readily uploaded

In summary, the wiki was considered suitable for the purposes of the My-Place, MyMusic research project for two reasons. First, it met the requirements of the community of participating researchers, as highlighted in the previous section, and second, it facilitated multimodal research processes by promoting research as a collaborative practice.

However, the wiki construction process required more than simply the selection of predesigned architectural aspects. First, we needed to select the most suitable software from among the many most popular options, which included, at the time, UseModWiki, MediaWiki, PhpWiki, TikiWiki, DokuWiki, WikkaWiki, MoinMoin, and OpenWiking. We decided to employ the Wikipedia package, MediaWiki, because we thought it would be easier for the community members to identify with the format and the way it functions. While developing the wiki framework, we decided it was necessary to establish a common file nomenclature for the existing data. A data unification solution was deployed. Our next decision concerned the look and feel of the wiki. We opted for the cleanest and clearest alternative, a predesigned version that felt more like a website than a wiki at first sight.

We used two criteria to organize the information and data. First, the home page featured an image and a title for each of the three main sections that coincided with the three main types of data collected (videos, pictures, and information). As shown in Figure 2.2, each item had a direct link to another page containing a list of the contributing countries. In all cases, the selected item (video, picture, or different kinds of information documents) could be seen online, saving time, effort, and space on the participants' personal computers, as there was no need for downloading. We found YouTube software to be the most effective for downsizing video clips. By creating our own private YouTube channel, we were also able to upload and convert videos, and then download them again for eventual transfer to the wiki. This easy way of handling uploaded mixed-mode data is identified by Jenkins (2006) as "transmedia navigation," where texts, photos, and video clips can be chunked, selected, copied, pasted, juxtaposed, and compared. This process enables researchers to scan across multimodal data to look for the emergence of similarities and patterns that can lead to themes and interpretations. We consider this to be one of the most useful and effective research processes that the wiki could provide. Second, the home page also had tabs leading to other kinds of data. These included ethical consent forms from every country, the protocol, a list of participants and their links, an editable reference list, and so on. This is how the wiki was first set up, but it was flexible, so that the dynamics of participation could later alter it.

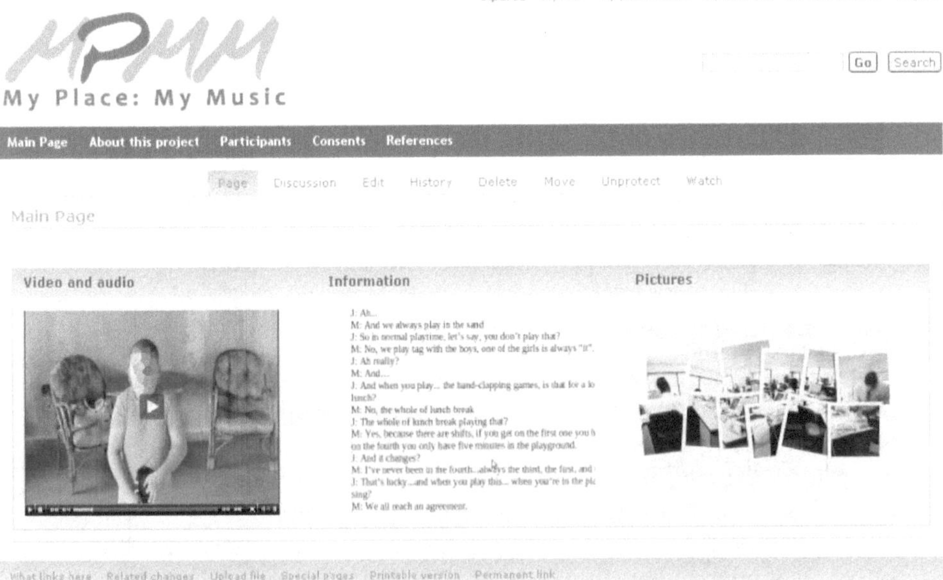

Figure 2.2. Opening page of the MyPlace, MyMusic Wiki.

Thus a wiki is a dynamic, alive, and processual resource that is continually evolving. Hyperlinks to other sites containing relevant information could be included when and where appropriate, and theoretical material (mainly articles) containing certain emerging interpretations could be uploaded. Turkle (1995) identifies the main characteristic of the internet as nonlinear, associative thinking supported by lots of information in small snippets, linking together and starting to form patterns. She argues that associative thinking is a powerful mental process that can be applied to the creative process of interpretive research, thanks to the capabilities of the wiki architecture. The way we tinker—bottom-up" rather than "top-down"—with the online data results is what Turkle (1995) refers to as a kind of "soft mastery," in which thinkers tend toward negotiation and compromise as opposed to the competition and dominance that is inherent, she suggests, in hierarchical, individualistic thought. It is at this point that associative thinking as an individual process of working with online data merges with "soft mastery," helping to engender the collaborative sharing of ideas, as seen in the next section.

After checking that the wiki was useful for our needs and purposes, we proceeded to buy a domain and look for a web hosting service to launch it. Because of the strict confidentiality of the data, access to the wiki was restricted to the researchers actively participating in the project who were each designated a personal password. The wiki manager uploaded some of the data and invited all researchers to follow suit, uploading their own data. We provided a sandbox where the users could test out and experiment with the wiki syntax, editing conventions and exploring other features and functionalities (Bean and Hott, 2005). There was obviously a learning curve for each wiki user that varied depending on that user's level of expertise, interest, and motivation. The version control system in the wiki settings can be used to reverse a change when necessary, which encouraged the less competent participants as well as the wiki manager.

Knowledge Creation through Collaborative Innovation

As discussed earlier, a wiki is not only a repository for managing multimedia data but also a virtual social space where knowledge can be actively constructed (Kolbitsch and Maurer, 2006). Another advantage of the wiki is that the knowledge construction process can be made visible to others, annotated, and discussed in the mediated dialogue that the wiki as a social space allows.[2]

For the research team, the wiki provided more than a space for collective gathering of information. The concept of "We-Think" proposed by Leadbeater (2008) illustrates what we, as a team, carried out: active processes of knowledge creation through collaborative innovation. As two of us wrote in an earlier article, "the interpretative dimension of research has always involved a creative process and creativity *can* be highly collaborative, a cumulative and social activity in which people with different viewpoints, different skills and different insights share and develop ideas together" (Young and Pérez, 2012, p. 8). We argued that research is generally conceived as an individual process and that researchers are less accustomed to this notion of ideas arising from dynamic processes of creative interaction generated by people who contribute diverse but potentially integrative ideas and insights. I will return to this idea later.

According to Leadbeater (2008), individuals participating in the collaborative activity receive recognition for the worth of their contributions. These three concepts, participation, collaboration, and recognition, are the three vertices that allow the notion of "We-Think," as a figurative triangle, to be operational.

Participation

Although theories from social science suggest that the social dynamics of community life itself should foster the desire to participate in social settings, it is not so straightforward in online communities (Gears, 2011; Parameswaran and Whinston, 2007b). Several studies of participation in social media platforms show very little real involvement. For example, Nelson (2006, quoted by Gears, 2011) drew on the 90:9:1 theory to illustrate that 90 percent of users were only lurkers,

9 percent contributed occasionally with comments, and only 1 percent contributed on a regular basis.

In our case, the MyPlace, MyMusic online community was different because the majority of the researchers already knew each other and others had met at the conference where the project had been born. Nonetheless, growth of participation in the wiki was slow. Patience and an understanding of each participant's work style were needed. It was also necessary to send e-mails from time to time to remind researchers of what needed to be done. We agree with Gears (2011) that the adoption of a wiki is slow as a workplace resource. As she also states, we found that the longer a wiki exists, the more users become active participants.

Recognition

Recognition from others can, however, provide a motivation for establishing and maintaining participation. In the MyPlace, MyMusic project, initial recognition was based on the collection of data from children and uploading the data to the wiki so that all the researchers could access it. The team completed this first step relatively quickly: visibility was important. From then on, posting on the forums and adding interpretative discussion notes was valued by other members of the team in the form of replies to the contributions. This created circular feedback, starting again with an entry from an author, which could call for the intervention of other researchers.

Collaboration

As described earlier, wikis are fertile spaces where collaboration is possible in new ways. Accordingly, it is important to examine aspects such as quality and egalitarianism as part of this study. The fact that the knowledge is created collaboratively by means of discussion makes for reasonably accurate information. In 2005 a study on the accuracy of Wikipedia was carried out by comparing its content with that found in the *Encyclopaedia Britannica*. It was discovered that some entries in Wikipedia contained errors but that this was the exception rather than the rule (Giles, 2005). This gives the online encyclopedia credibility and makes it a reliable source of information that can be used without skepticism.

Furthermore, the collaboration involved in a wiki can foster an egalitarianism that contrasts with academic settings, where there can be a very clear hierarchy. Everyone on our team, from senior to junior researchers, from PhDs to graduate students, had a voice that was equally valued. Wiki dynamics can encourage democratic interaction, suggesting that technologically mediated processes may facilitate changes in conventional conceptions of academic knowledge production (Young, Ilari, and Pérez, 2010).[3] One of these changes counters the traditional belief that the creation of knowledge is an individual pursuit (for more information, see Young and Pérez, 2012). Moreover, it has been suggested that studies conducted by a group of experts can result in their being planned from a more holistic viewpoint and their ability to achieve more accurate results (e.g., Gillen and Cameron, 2010).

Considerations, Challenges, and Further Directions of Research

After setting up the main part of the MyPlace, MyMusic wiki we were able to focus on secondary but equally important issues that arose during the process and gave us "food for thought." While we were designing and setting up the wiki, we realized that the dividing line between work and leisure was sometimes blurred. We were uploading data, deciding how to present it, selecting our headlines and other details. During this process we were reminded more of the enjoyment derived from maintaining our walls on social networking sites such as Facebook rather than the routine, often somewhat mundane tasks involved in collating and preparing data for a conventional research project. Moreover, we also found ourselves wanting to visit the wiki on a daily basis: to check what was new, maybe to see what the Greek child looked like, make a quick trip to a Spanish garden, get a glimpse of the Brazilian children's bedrooms, or find out how many hours of music education were compulsory in each country. This is why as early as in the first public presentation of the MyPlace, MyMusic wiki, we coined the concept of "serious play" (Pérez and Young, 2010) to refer to this situation in which creative activity merges with professional output. The "serious play" side of technology-enhanced research processes suggests a fruitful topic for further study.

Another discovery is that while contributing to the wiki we had to be careful to use the right tone when intervening with others and, at the same time, find a common, clear language to express our opinions and tackle shared interests together. In other words, we had to reach an agreement on a kind of online "etiquette." The colloquial short comments or ironic remarks that we would use on Facebook or Twitter would not have been appropriate, but neither would the formal, academic style of prose found in books and papers (Young and Pérez, 2012). We aimed for a clear, concise style of commenting. In addition, because the team was made up of researchers of different nationalities, we also had to carefully consider the issue of cultural sensitivity in the styles of communication and the communicative roles that emerged. As several authors have pointed out (Bolam et al., 2005; Cassidy et al., 2008; Young and Pérez, 2012), when working collaboratively with colleagues and giving feedback, there is a need for a high level of trust, respect, and humility.

Another small point that is worth highlighting is the amount of stationery the wiki saved the team and the consequent reduction in our carbon footprint. Inadvertently, we became more eco-conscious because of the reduced need to travel and meet face-to-face to manage the project. Even if data from a first batch of CDs and DVDs were uploaded by one "central" researcher, all subsequent data were uploaded directly from the original recording devices. We are proud to have been able to work with an eco-friendly research medium that eliminates the need for stationery and traveling.

Conclusions

The main characteristics of the wiki—its simplicity, flexibility, affordability, accessibility, and usability—made it an essential part of the MyPlace, MyMusic project. The implementation of the wiki was critical to the flow of communication among the team members, allowing participatory research and long-distance interaction while, we believe, considerably enhancing the research processes and methods.

During the early days of the project we realized the wiki's potential. What was initially established as a simple tool to support the project gave rise to ideas and new frontiers for research. Its adoption made us reflect on key ideas of democratic research, online etiquette in research collaborations, "serious play," and eco-friendly research. The MyPlace, MyMusic wiki opened up an exciting new dimension for our research. It fostered idea sharing, along with cooperation and collaboration among researchers with a common goal of creating knowledge together. By making individual contributions to a forum as experts on a topic, and then allowing others to view and criticize those contributions, we also empowered our research community, making it stronger as a whole.

Acknowledgments

I dedicate this chapter to Susan Young who so energetically planned and developed the MyPlace, MyMusic project and who is a real inspiration to me. Also, I would like to thank Marcel Soleda for his technical advice and assistance.

Notes

1. Although this chapter is written by one author, the decisions made and some of the ideas presented were the fruits of teamwork, hence the shifts from singular to plural form when appropriate.

2. The default discussion section consists of a simple open box that can then be difficult to follow because the sequence of entries and responses is not organized. Like Wolff (2009), we decided to add a forum (Extension AWC Forum from MediaWiki) where all the researchers could share their thoughts, ask each other questions about the data, and possibly start to work on coauthored articles.

3. See Young and Pérez (2012) for information about the challenges involved in adopting a wiki to underpin creative and democratic research.

SECTION II

Thematic Interpretations

3 Public and Secret Musical Worlds of Children

Claudia Gluschankof

CHARLIE (UK): When it's the morning and they're [her older brother, her parents] not awake, I play a musical thing with my teddies.

FATHER: You've got a musical game with teddies have you?

CHARLIE: Yeah, it's a secret, but it doesn't matter.

INTERVIEWER: Well, don't tell us any secrets.

CHARLIE: It doesn't matter—I've let it go now.

PLAYING A MUSICAL "thing" with her teddies at home is the well-kept secret of Charlie (the British girl), which she let go, probably without planning it, during the interview. What is she telling us through this secret? Is Charlie the only one among the children in the project that had a musical secret? Even if some or most of them had musical secrets, are those lived only within their life at home or also in their musical lives out of the home?

Corsaro (2011) suggests that preadolescent children, that is, seven to thirteen years old, "often separate themselves from others through the sharing of secrets. Sharing secrets includes . . . the production of complex texts and artifacts" (p. 238). Is it possible to include musical experiences and artifacts among these secrets? This chapter explores the several cultures in which the MyPlace, MyMusic children lived at home and outside the home, the ways they negotiated their musical lives, and the interaction between the cultures, in a search to discover the children's private and secret musical lives, if they existed as such.

Conceptual Framework

Culture has been defined in a variety of ways. In one of its definitions, the Merriam-Webster (2000) dictionary terms it as "the customary beliefs, social forms, and material traits of a racial, religious, or social group." Corsaro (2011, p. 118) presents a functionalist definition of culture as "shared values, beliefs, and artifacts" (p. 118) and a cognitive one: "a set of organizing principles that people keep in their heads and that guide behavior."

Children are members of society, and therefore they actively participate in the production and reproduction of rituals and artifacts. Nevertheless, they "most often occupy subordinate positions and are exposed to much more cultural information than they can process and understand . . . it is an important assumption of the interpretive approach that important features of peer cultures arise and develop as a result of children's attempts to make sense of, and to a certain extent to resist, the adult world" (Corsaro, 1997, p. 96).

Children's cultures are the focus of study in fields such as the Anthropology of Childhood (e.g., Montgomery, 2009), Childhood Studies (e.g., James, Jenks, and Prout, 1998) and the Sociology of Childhood (e.g., Corsaro, 2011). Children's cultures make reference to the adults' cultures in which children live but also to the cultures children develop by themselves, and all these are interwoven (Corsaro, 2003). One type of child-developed culture is among peer groups, which, as with any peer culture is characterized by its being "public, collective, and performative" (Geertz, 1973; Goffman, 1974 in Corsaro, 2011, p. 120). Corsaro (2003) maintains that children's peer cultures "have an autonomy that makes them worthy of documentation and study in their own right" (p. 5). But do children develop other cultures that are not peer cultures, that is, are not public and collective? What about the individual worlds of children at home, especially in middle-class families, where children have their own rooms and can enjoy some autonomy there? Do children develop their own culture in the privacy of their home? In this project, the children's musical cultures, presented at home by the children and their parents, are considered worthy of documentation and study in their own right, to look for the public and the private in them.

Corsaro and Eder (1990) focused their studies on children's peer cultures defined as "a stable set of activities or routines, artifacts, values, and concerns that children produce and share in interaction with their peers" (p. 197). The cultures that they studied develop within educational settings, where children engage mainly in face-to-face interactions, in a complex context formally controlled and shaped by adults (e.g., classrooms, assemblies), and informally designed and controlled by children such as playgrounds and hallways (Boocock and Scott, 2005). These children's cultures are embedded in the adults' culture, and they interact and influence each other. This type of relationship recalls somehow Bronfenbrenner's (1979) ecosystems, which refer to the variety of environments or settings in which the individual acts. These systems are dynamic and are reshaped by the individuals, at the same time that the individuals are influenced by these systems. In an earlier paper I proposed this type of model as a framework for interpreting the musical cultures of young children (Gluschankof, 2009).

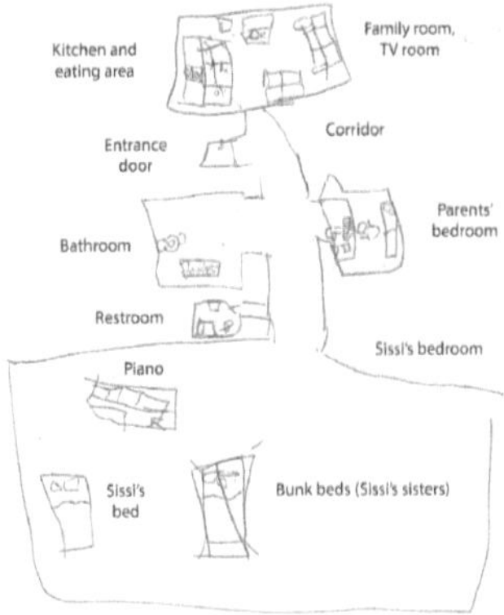

Figure 3.1. Images of four visited homes: Greece (top, left), United Kingdom (top, right), Kenya (bottom, left), Israel (bottom, right: sketch of the home by Sissi, the child participant from Israel).

Children's peer cultures develop in educational settings but they contribute to the other cultures in which they are embedded, including the worlds of family and home. The question is, if children's peer cultures are developed in educational settings, does a child's culture in general, and specifically a musical one, also develop at home? Do children participate in cultural production and reproduction at home, not always under parents' control or even with their parents' knowledge? The vignette opening this chapter may offer a hint to answering these questions. Charlie's father does not seem to be aware of his daughter's secret. Is this secret and private world Charlie's way of making sense of or resisting the adult world? Accessing educational settings in order to study children's culture seems to be much easier than accessing families. The consequence is that we know more about children's peer cultures, the public and shared ones, than the cultures that develop within the children's private lives. This chapter focuses on the latter.

Children's musical cultures at school have been studied by researchers who can access educational settings relatively easily. Such studies have focused on the informal contexts designed and controlled by children. Campbell (1998) focused on school bus rides, halls, and lunch breaks; Marsh (2009) on playground culture; and Gluschankof (2005) on kindergarten children's musical culture during free play. Because gaining access to homes is more difficult, the study of children's home culture presents researchers with certain challenges. Arguably, each home is different and affords children different opportunities to engage with music, and this includes both the physical structure of a house and family structure. Figure 3.1 depicts images of four of the homes visited.

Within the home, it would seem that babies and toddlers, who depend on their parents, are easier to study, since the focus is typically on the relationship between the caregiver and child. Examples include Mackinlay (2012), who wrote an auto-ethnography on musical aspects of her motherhood experience; Addessi (2009), who studied musical routines in the care of babies in Italy; and Young and Gillen (2010), who studied musical experiences during a day in the life of toddlers in seven different countries. Studying the musical lives of older children at home is more difficult because they are active in the construction and negotiation of their musical lives among several worlds, in and out of school and family (Griffin, 2011).

Children's Musical Worlds

The common research protocol specified that each child be asked to sing and to "show and tell" what music-related things s/he has at home. Their choices, as shown in the recorded performances and the interviews, have the potential to inform us about their musical worlds as they wanted to share them with us, and sometimes the ways that their parents understood or misunderstood them. Because the children were asked to sing and "show and tell," these interpretations are presented separately in the following sections.

Singing Their Worlds

The children's chosen repertoire included mainly songs learned at school (Maria in Spain, Brad and Rose in the United States, Melina in Greece, Basje and Rosa in the Netherlands, Maiara in Brazil, and Sissi in Israel) and pop songs from adult or youth culture (Giovani in Brazil, Christine in Singapore, Rose, Melina, Basje, and Annie in Taiwan). It also included singing games usually played with peers (Maria in Spain), pop songs for children learned from CDs and DVDs (Charlie in the UK, Annie), and songs learned and usually performed at Sunday school and church (Michael in Kenya). The song repertoire—unsurprisingly—reflects the variety of cultures to which children belong: school formal, school informal, family, wider society. The interesting aspect is the way that the children performed those songs.

Songs belonging to the school repertoire were performed mostly in a soft voice, in an introverted and a somehow inexpressive way (i.e., without dynamics changes, without stressing words, with an unchanging facial expression), as Michael did when he sang "Mary Had a Little Lamb" and Melina did when she sang "Prince Lemon and Queen Onion." The singing was accompanied by gestures if that was the way they learned the songs at school. Such was the case of Brad, who sang the school repertoire with hand signs (the school music program is Kodály-based), and was happy to demonstrate "Here Comes the Bluebird" with his mother and the researcher forming a small circle. When he moved to the recording of a children's song in pop style, he showed much more enthusiasm. The difference in the performance may reside in the motivation to learn the song (extrinsic in the case of school repertoire, and intrinsic in the songs learned at home), in the meaning the songs carry for the children, and even in the music styles. Basje in the Netherlands sang the action song "Doe je handen omhoog" (in English, "Put your hands up"), standing up, moving her body, and showing some embarrassment. Head voice production featured in most of the performances of this type of repertoire, as in the case of Sissi. Head voice also featured in Christine's singing accompanied by her father playing the piano. Her singing can be considered Western art music style. She looked very conscious of her voice production, did not smile, and her facial expressions were minimal as she sang "Tomorrow" from *Annie, the Musical*, and "Oh Danny Boy."

If songs learned in what Campbell (1998) defines as highly structured ways were performed rather inexpressively and softly, then songs learned in enculturated ways, that is, naturally and without formal instruction, were performed in very different ways. Those songs were all in Western pop style, either composed for children or belonging to the adult culture. Children in the project learned them from a variety of media (e.g., CDs and DVDs) and performed them in an extroverted style and with enthusiasm, as Rose did singing "Swinging on a Star," the American pop standard. Charlie sang "Robot Parade," a song included in *No!* the first album of music for children released by the alternative American rock band They Might Be Giants (TMBG) (*No!*, 2012). She sang it very confidently, holding her toy microphone in her hand, adding movements related to the lyrical content and the musical style.

Basje was very fond of Celine Dion, the Canadian singer, and performed her song "A New Day Has Come," standing up, rather fluently, swinging slightly, imitating the singer's production, limited by his own vocal skills: the higher pitches sounded very clear, but the lower pitches were almost inaudible. Christine's way of performing the pop song was very different from the ways she performed the songs her father accompanied. She sang along with the ABBA (the

English-singing Swedish pop group) recording of the song "I Have a Dream," during a car ride. She knew most of the words, and sang them in full volume, but the low pitches were too low for her. She solved this difficulty, as Basje did, by singing them softly. The children's appropriation of pop songs seemed to be an expression of "middle-class teens' and preteens' increasing desires to look and act 'grown up'" (Cook and Kaiser, 2004, p. 208).

Giovani also chose a pop song to sing along: "Ai de ti Copacabana" (in English, something like "Watch out, Copacabana"), joining Alceu Valença (a Brazilian folk-song writer, of whom Giovani's elder brother is very fond). Although he sang the entire song, his singing was not very clear, but he obviously knew all the lyrics because sometimes he was ahead of the singer. His mother suggested that he hold the recorder as if it were a microphone. At the beginning he was very shy, but later he seemed more relaxed and included some dancing in his performance. The shyness may be explained by the fact that Giovani followed his mother's suggestion. Although Melina defied her mother and elder brother, choosing to sing "Emeis i dyo san ena" (in English, "The two of us"), a song by Michalis Hatzigiannis, a famous Greek Cypriot pop singer, she could not overcome her shyness. Giovani did overcome it when he sang a parody of a traditional song on his own initiative, challenging his mother's desires: "Jingle bell, jingle bell acabou o papel" (in English, "Jingle bell, Jingle bell, I'm running out of paper").[1] He performed it in a happily extroverted way, thus defying the adults' control and taking control of the situation as preadolescents do (Corsaro, 2010).

Extroversion and introversion seem to reside more in the children's control of their performance than in the music style, and can be seen as an expression of their construction of their own lives, "forming independent 'social relationships and culture'" (James, 2011, p. 41). This is especially clear in Christine's rap version of "Tomorrow" from the musical *Annie*. She sang it during a car ride, integrating and demonstrating her knowledge of both the original song (performed in Western art music style to the accompaniment of her father) and the rap style. She sang it in a very extroverted way, very expressively, varying the dynamics and building up to a crescendo toward the end. In other words, she transformed the song taught by her father into a new one that showed not only her understanding of it but also her challenging of the adult world as represented by her parents. This act of challenge, though, was not performed in front of her father, and not in the place assigned by the adult members of the family to perform music. She chose or found a situation where her father was not present (she was riding with her mother to pick up her father), and her mother was busy driving. Maiara also chose to perform in a safe place, where she could exercise control and agency. She invited the fieldworker to her "private" place, where she sang her favorite song, belonging to her school repertoire: "Feliz da primavera" ("Happy from spring"; by an unknown composer) and "Sabiá" (by Lydio Roberto, a Brazilian songwriter), as

Feliz da Primavera & Sabiá

Unknown composer & Lydio Roberto

Happy from Spring & Sabiá

Beautiful flowers will arrive with spring
Lillies, Daffodils will sing with spring
Lillies, daffodils and rosemary
Violets and jasmines.

The sun will shine
Birds will sing with spring
Beautiful flowers will arrive with spring.

Fly sabiá (bird), fly, come sing
Fly sabiá, fly sabiá, fly sabiá
Bring a flower on your beak
Rose, camellia or jasmine
Bring a flower on your beak like this
Rose, camellia or jasmine

Beautiful flowers will arrive with spring
Lillies, Daffodils will sing with spring
Lillies, daffodils and rosemary
Violets and jasmines.

Figure 3.2. Score for combined version of "Feliz da primavera" (anonymous) and Sabiá (Lydio Roberto) as sung by Maiara in Brazil. Sabiá excerpt printed courtesy of composer Lydio Roberto.

depicted in Figure 3.2. She sang it in a way that seemed to be the "official version" learned at school, while touching flowers, bouncing, with a very soft, head voice. When she sang about the birds she added what seemed to be the agreed gesture for it (joining her two hands to indicate flying). The way the performance continued was surprising and hints at her agency: she continued singing with the same words, but improvising the rather long melody, finishing with an ending that was clearly marked by the gesture, the *ritenuto* and the melodic turn, although she did not finish on the tonic. The performance lasted almost three minutes. She sang it later, in a shorter version. Maiara also improvised when she agreed to sing a popular children's song, originally from Colombia ("Ya lloviendo está" ["It's raining"]), in its Brazilian Portuguese version. She related to the song as basic material for her improvisation; she changed tempi, introduced some melodic turns, used a variety of articulations, and added gestures, ending clearly with a diminuendo and a shy gesture. Maiara's mother talked about the importance of play in her daughter's life, but did not mention her singing improvisation.

Rosa told the interviewer that she sings songs that she invents by herself when she is in her room, but she did not share any of those with the interviewer, and it seems that her parents were not aware of this either, as expressed in the mother's interview: "The only one here who is really singing is Rosa. The whole day. She is singing or talking. The whole day through. You can see when she has learned a song at school, she reproduces it at home."

Catherine's mother did not mention that her daughter pretends to sing, as Catherine told the interviewer "when my friends are at my place we often sing into it [the toy microphone], when we're pretending that we're singing." Brad said that he likes to sing around the house and that he always has a song playing in his head, and his parents added that they hear him singing at night. Singing has already been identified in young children's play and in situations when they are by themselves, such as lying in bed, and bath time. This singing is integrated into their play (Bjørkvold, 1989/1992; Young, 2006), and is comforting in some situations, serving as company (Gluschankof, 2005), and at times is a means of self-entertainment or self-regulation (Campbell, 1998). Catherine's, Maiara's, Brad's and Rosa's singing accounts also reveal the existence of activities and places that are not known to their parents, and may hint at the existence of a secret and private musical world.

Playing (with) Instruments

"The introduction of an object or artefact into an interview context can dramatically impact on the process of joint meaning-making, serving as an effective joint referent" (Westcott and Littleton, 2005, p. 148). This was done through the showing of anything that children considered music-related and important to them.

Most of them mentioned melodic and harmonic instruments (e.g., guitar, piano, electronic keyboard), and only after the interviewers continued asking, and with the interviewer's or the parents' help, talked about other instruments:

SISSI: O.K. . . . a lot, like . . . a lot of recorders . . . piano . . . guitar . . . well . . . [confers privately with her mother].

MOM: We have musical instruments from all over the world, so that's also called a musical instrument.

INTERVIEWER: I will ask a question about music right away. Do you have a musical instrument?

BASJE: Hmmmm no.

INTERVIEWER: No? Nothing at all?

BASJE: Only toy instruments.

Charlie had prepared all her "musical things" on the floor of her bedroom: her teddy bear that played a music-box-like tune (the Lullaby by Brahms); a tiny music box; a violin; a "magical" plastic drum; shakers; and a toy microphone. The other children presented what they considered to be musical instruments. Maybe the difference resides in the way the interviewers asked the children, and not in the children's perception of musical instruments.

Children differed not only in what they considered to be musical instruments or "musical things" but also in the way they showed and played them. Keyboard instruments had a strong presence: Rosa, Sissi, Christine, Brad, and Rose agreed to play the piano, all of them playing from a music score. The repertoire varied from very basic beginners' pieces as in the case of Rosa, through children's songs as Sissi played ("Yemey hachanuka," a popular Hannukah folk song), folk songs (Brad played "Good King Wenceslas"), and classical music (Brad played the theme from Haydn's "Surprise" Symphony, and Christine played Beethoven's "Für Elise"). Their playing ranged from unintelligible (Rosa) to fluid playing with few mistakes (Christine). Sissi chose to play a known song, although her mother said that "she really enjoys experimenting with the instrument, to discover." Maybe for Sissi experimentation is not something to show others or to have documented.

Giovani, Michael, Catherine, and Melina showed and played their electronic keyboards. The boys played recognizable songs. Michael did so by reading from a beginner's book but also tried playing "Mary Had a Little Lamb" by ear, and succeeding. When he played traditional instruments (a drum and a traditional string instrument he called a "guitar," which resembles a traditional African harp), he did it in the traditional way, without reading any notation, and repeating the same patterns very skillfully on the drum. Giovani also followed the notation included in the keyboard package. This was based on the names of the keys, which his mother wrote on the keys. He also played "Mary Had a Little Lamb" and later "Jingle Bells." Giovani and Michael each played Brazilian instruments, also without reading any notation. Catherine and Melina played using the automatic features of the electronic keyboard, pressing keys without intending to play a known song or an identifiable melody.

The keyboard playing of the children reflected, as did their singing, their ways of learning the instrument: those who studied the instrument in highly structured ways played with two hands from conventional notation, performing pieces of their own culture or classical pieces. Those who were taught by relatives, who were neither teachers nor experts, played well-known English children's songs, not precisely from their own culture, but songs that belong to a global repertoire used in electronic toys. What about Melina and Catherine? They explored all the possibilities of the keyboard, not just the keys, as if it were a piano, and also the effects of the other function keys. The first stage of getting to know any musical instrument in all its aspects, and not only musically, is to explore all its possibilities. This stage has been widely reported and studied among preschool children in preschool settings (Cohen, 1980; Delalande, 2009; Moorhead, Sandvik, and Wight, 1951/1978; Swanwick and Tillman, 1986). Free musical play at school has not been a focus of study either in educational settings or at home, so the present study may indicate that exploration is a necessary stage in getting to know any instrument, regardless of age or setting.

Maybe those not taking lessons felt free to explore the instruments. This phenomenon was identified in the case of the violin as well: Brad, who takes lessons, played "Twinkle, Twinkle Little Star," whereas Charlie who owns a violin, but has not yet started taking lessons, plucked some strings and rubbed the bow on the strings. Exploration was also the main characteristic of the way children showed and played the toy and world instruments, including glockenspiel, hand drums, cymbals, toy trumpet, and toy roll-up piano (Brad); castanets, maracas, *samba ballen* (shakers), triangle, colorful toy xylophone, tambourine, sleigh bells, woodblock, harmonica, recorder, *djembe* (Basje); rain stick, maracas, various shakers, a variety of flutes, and *mbira* (Sissi).

The way children showed and played the different instruments is interesting but not surprising—influences from the adult world were clear in the way the children related to the instruments, including their doubts about what could be considered a musical instrument. The interviews included information about what children did with instruments when their parents were not around, and that gives us a glimpse into the children's private, and sometimes secret, musical worlds.

Sissi's mother is aware that her daughter plays with her instruments: "Those instruments aren't for [my] work. People know that I like [musical instruments], so they collect them for me, and this is a bunch that someone—that my brother brought me. And what happens, really: every time I go looking, I suddenly discover that they've disappeared, and then I understood that [Sissi] takes them. I find them hidden here, underneath all sorts of [stuff]." Sissi herself said that she takes the instrument bag from her Daddy's room to her bedroom (which she shares with her older sisters) or outdoors, where she plays with them by herself or with friends. Catherine also mentioned playing with friends and "musical things"—"when I and my friends are at my place we often sing into it [a microphone], when we're pretending that we're singing." And Maria said, "We take the instruments we've got at home and pretend to play them . . . [the drum]. It's for when my best friend comes round, and my cousins, to play with sometimes. When other friends come too . . . we play with it." Based on these accounts, musical instruments function as cultural artifacts of preadolescent girls' peer culture.

Conclusions

The research tools, interviewing the child while s/he sings, the "show and tell," and interviewing the parent, revealed the children's musical cultures at home, which include both secret and private worlds. Parents are acquainted with the public world, which they believe is the only one their children live in. Such is the case of Sissi's mother, who explained that her daughter "really loves the songs of the choir. She simply told you that she doesn't want this choir; she's determined about this." The gap between the mother's beliefs about her daughter's preferences and Sissi's declared preferences, both as presented in the interview and in the performed songs, may be an expression of challenging the adult authority, as preadolescent children do (Corsaro, 1997). It may also present the difference between the public world, a world shared with the adults, and the child's private world, or as Charlie said her secret one. This private world includes singing pop songs, songs primarily aimed at an older audience, learned in enculturated ways, out of intrinsic motivation. It also includes producing sounds from artifacts that are not considered musical instruments as well as exploring and playing musical instruments in nonconventional ways.

Children's public musical world is one dominated by adults as facilitators, mediators, and agents. In their private and secret worlds, children are agents of their own musical experiences. Children negotiate their musical worlds, both public and private/secret, by reproducing adult ways of performing, if the repertoire has been taught by adults. But they also transform the repertoire when adults are not focusing their attention on them; playing musical instruments and also playing with "musical things"; sharing with the family, but also playing in the privacy of bedrooms, or "secret hideaways" and during secret games. Both worlds are the safe spaces to experience the inherent tensions of preadolescence.

Note

1. Editors' note: This song (and the parody sung by Giovani) is well-known by Brazilian children and often sung in English. The words "I'm running out of paper" allude to being out of toilet paper. The song is frequently sung by school-age children as a way to capture teachers' (or adults') attention, in that it represents a form of transgression.

4 Belonging and Identity

Exploring Gendered Meanings of Musicking in Seven-Year-Olds

Elizabeth Andang'o and
Caroline Brendel Pacheco

The windows on children's musical experiences in the home that we gathered in this project offer some insights into the way children learn to see themselves, to know their position in the world in relation to others, and to feel a sense of belonging to a certain social class, ethnicity, and gender. In this chapter we explore how music offers a set of experiences through which "our" children could make sense of themselves as boys or girls.

How gender and musical identities inform one another within the specific context of the home interested us as we looked across all the project data. How does the child's gender shape their musicking (Small, 1998), and how do the possibilities for musical experiences available to them in the home constrain or facilitate the formation of their gender identity? There are many different components and forms of participation within music that might carry symbolic gendered meanings: musical instruments; technologies that enable forms of musical participation; the music itself in the form of songs and instrumental pieces; and the performance of music through singing or playing. In this chapter we consider these different aspects of musicking in our exploration of gendered meanings.

In a chapter focusing on gender in musical identity, Dibben (2002) has discussed some central and sometimes controversial issues concerning gender identity and music. Her review revealed that boys' and girls' own gender development can influence their musical perceptions: girls often see themselves as good singers, for example, whereas boys have more confidence in composition. This gender distinction exists not only in musical performance and composition but also in musical taste; preferences for specific styles seem to influence and be influenced by children's evolving gender identity.

The practices of appropriate musical behavior reflect attitudes about gender that are widely shared in a society. In some societies these may be overt—for example, specific rules about who can or cannot use or see or touch certain instruments or who may perform certain styles or genres of music. In other societies the gender "rules" may be less overt and scholars have worked to reveal the "hidden" gender biases that lie behind instrument choice, the use of music, musical tastes and preferences, and performances of music. Researchers, particularly from a feminist orientation, have sought to reveal asymmetries that limit the opportunities available to girls—and also to boys (Green, 2002).

An important strand of academic research has explored the connotations of gender embedded in instrument choice and participation in musical performance. The main aim of this work was to inform educational practice, but here we borrow the research to shed light on our children's choices and uses of musical instruments in the home.

Gender and Instrument Choice

Research has revealed that children and adolescents stereotype musical instruments as either "masculine" or "feminine" (see Dibben, 2002). In a 1996 study, O'Neill and Boulton found that British children between nine and ten years old displayed gender differences in their instrument preference, with boys preferring drums, guitar, and trumpet, and girls preferring flute, piano, and violin. Harrison and O'Neill (2000) repeated the study with seven- to eight-year-olds and found exactly the same results. Marshall and Shibazaki (2013) discovered that even among three- and four-year-olds the same gender stereotyping occurred. Moreover, the attribution of instruments to one gender or the other is resistant to change. Researchers presented gender-consistent (i.e., female playing flute, male playing drums) and gender-inconsistent role models in concerts to children in the anticipation that role modeling might change the instrument preferences. However, contrary to expectations, the concerts had a negative effect: children responded less well to concerts played by the gender-inconsistent musicians. For example, when girls saw male violinists or pianists, their interest in these instruments decreased (Harrison and O'Neill, 2000).

Looking across all the children in the project, their choices of instruments seemed to conform to the predictions of preference found by O'Neill and Boulton (2001). Boys presented performances on percussion instruments, while girls continued to choose the flute, violin, and the piano. Table 4.1 depicts "our" children's choice of musical instruments, when informed.

Giovani in Brazil had been playing drums from early on, beginning in preschool, an educational institution that children attend typically between the ages of two and five years. Although most of the instruments he has since played are varied, he played his brother's *divino* drum (medium-size drum played with two drumsticks) and attempted to play the *pandeiro* (i.e., a type of hand frame drum

Table 4.1. Musical instruments played by children who took part in the MyPlace, MyMusic project.

Child's pseudonym	Country of origin	Gender	Instruments
Charlie	UK	Female	Violin (she owns one but has not started playing it)
Basje	Netherlands	Male	Not indicated
Rosa	Netherlands	Female	Piano
Michael	Kenya	Male	Drums, piano, and recorder
Giovani	Brazil	Male	Drums and Brazilian percussion instruments
Maiara	Brazil	Female	Recorder, guitar, and Brazilian percussion instruments
Giovanna	Brazil	Female	Recorder
Sissi	Israel	Female	Piano and cello
Brad	United States	Male	Violin and piano
Rose	United States	Female	No particular instrument, enjoys singing
Maria	Spain	Female	Guitar (she has just received the instrument on her birthday)
Annie	Taiwan	Female	Cello
Melina	Greece	Female	Toy guitar and piano
Christine	Singapore	Female	Piano, violin, and recorder
Catherine	Denmark	Female	Not indicated
Federico	Italy	Male	Specific instruments are not indicated, although it is reported that he plays (an) instrument at his grandparents' home
Anna	Italy	Female	Specific instruments are not indicated, although it is reported that she plays (an) instrument at her grandparents' home

popular in Brazil). However he found it easier to play the Brazilian *tamborim* (a smaller frame drum). He also showed some interest in playing the guitar, another "male preferred" instrument, but was not overly enthusiastic about it. Giovani's preference for "masculine" instruments seemed to be based on his father's and (much) older half-brother's influence, tempered by how often they allowed him to play their instruments. Family role models therefore play an important role in influencing children's musical choices and preferences, as we will see elsewhere in this chapter.

Choice of gender-appropriate instruments in childhood is also dependent on their availability to children, even from an early age. For Michael in Kenya, his parents recall his fascination as a toddler with the drum set at their local church: "We just observed that he had an interest in especially drums, as the [church] service was almost beginning . . . the next thing we would hear [was] bang!" This had prompted his parents to plan for future lessons in drums. However, the parents also noted his interest in drums and sought to encourage it, thus reinforcing a gender preference probably present in their own conceptions of appropriate musical boyhood. In the cases of both Giovani and Michael, parental influence (as well as siblings) may have encouraged choice of instruments based on gender stereotyping.

The girls in the study appeared to prefer orchestral instruments such as the flute and violin (Green, 1997). Charlie in the UK proudly pulled out the violin from under her bed and told of her ambition to start lessons soon. Annie in Taiwan would like to learn piano, another instrument preferred by girls (O'Neill and Boulton, 1996). However, through parental intervention, she was to start cello lessons instead. The girls nevertheless fell primarily within the selection of musical instruments that affirm and inscribe feminine musical behavior. Interestingly, Abeles and Porter (1978) found that the cello was not regarded with a significant gender association in the eyes of parents.

The example of Maiara would seem to be contradictory, since she had learned recorder and guitar at school, instruments she deems "easy to play." If the guitar is indeed considered a "male" instrument, the fact that she plays her mother's guitar indicates that a parental role model can intercept the gender stereotyping that may be associated with certain instruments. Tenenbaum and Leaper (2002) conducted a meta-analysis of forty-three studies investigating the relationship between parents' gender schemas and their offspring's gender-related cognitions. According to their findings, parental inclinations toward more traditional schemas resulted in offspring with gender-typed cognitions about themselves and others. In other words, there is a possible influence of parents on their children's gender-related thinking. The ages of the children in their study ranged from infant to early adulthood, making their findings relevant to this study. Maiara's mother has possibly influenced her departure from more gender-stereotyped musical instruments onto a different path. Furthermore, the guitar is a very popular instrument in Brazil, so many girls learn it from quite a young age.

Brad in the United States played instruments (violin and piano) generally associated with femininity. Analyzing older students' discourse, Green (2002) suggests that boys tend to suppress tastes or choices that seem to be feminine. Those who "interrupt femininity" to reaffirm their masculinity pursue "male" choices. On the other hand, those who do not abandon "feminine views" have to establish symbolic masculinity through other means. Because Brad started music lessons from a very young age, it is possible that his mother may have influenced his choices. The implication is that she chose the instruments he should play based on her own preferences. Thus, yet again, we see how parents are influential role models for young children in the process of musical gender socializing. Younger children may have some awareness of gender stereotyping of instruments, but have been found to be less influenced in their choice of instruments that carry connotations of masculinity or femininity (Abeles and Porter, 1978).

Looking across the project as whole, gender-based preferences for certain musical instruments do seem to be broadly upheld in the choices of instruments the children play. However, other factors also contributed, such as the role modeling of parents and siblings that may influence instrumental choice, the availability of certain instruments, and the age at which and the context in which the child first encountered them. In terms of playing orchestral and traditional instruments, "our" children at this age appeared to be still strongly oriented by their parents and the influence they bring to bear. This is, of course, partly a question of purchase of the instruments and lessons over which the parents still maintain control.

Gender and Singing

As discussed in the introduction to this volume, each child in the project was asked to sing his or her favorite song and knew that it would be recorded for others to listen to. There are two dimensions to consider here in relation to gender: the act of singing and the choice of song.

In exploring gender and singing a brief look at some cross-cultural and historical examples demonstrates the ways that songs and song-singing performance can carry gendered meanings. In some world traditions, the singing of certain songs supports cultural or gender hegemony, and in others, it is deemed a neutral activity, or more associated with females and hence to be avoided by males. In many African cultures, during musical performances, women mainly sing as an accompaniment to male instrumentalists (Campbell, 2006; Miller and Shahriari, 2009). The history of singing in Western society reveals that both men and women have engaged in it from the onset, yet in gender-appropriate ways. Female sing-

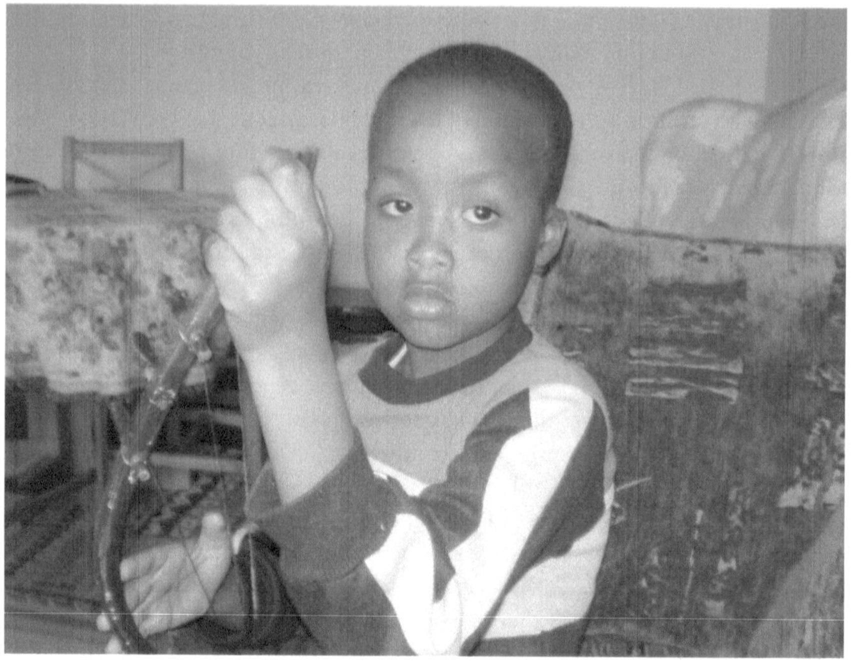

Figure 4.1. Picture of Michael in Kenya. Published with parental permission.

ing was accepted only in familiar situations; moreover, it was important that women played accompanying instruments, generally the piano and harp (O'Neill, 2002). Welch (2011) reported that female choristers were introduced into English cathedrals, a bastion of male-only singers for many centuries, only as recently as the late twentieth century. However, popular culture has raised the profile of singing as a masculine activity (Hall, 2005). It is interesting to note that with many male role models in the popular music industry, singing has risen phenomenally in profile.

In some cases, perhaps not surprisingly given the nature of the task, the children were hesitant to sing. It was noticeable, however, that the boys were more hesitant than the girls. Michael in Kenya (see Figure 4.1), for example, sung hesitantly, but when joined by his older sister, displayed greater confidence. Giovani in Brazil also felt shy singing in front of the camera, but finally relaxed and sang. Since these boys were able to overcome their uncertainty and then sing, we attributed their reluctance in part to the nature of the request. However, their hesitancy may reveal something significant about the gendered nature of singing. Stereotypically, boys find less affirmation of their masculinity in singing, although this may be drawn along quite specific lines of style and genre, with the emulation of male pop singers providing an opening where boys may find singing more identity affirming.

Brad in the United States, on the other hand, stood out as a confident singer. He was aware that he had a good singing voice "because my teacher says so," and said that he liked to sing around the house. Brad demonstrated excellent singing skills, nurtured both at home by his male parent modeling the activity and by a Kodály-based music program at school. Kodály programs aim to teach competence and confidence in singing. For Brad, singing carried positive connotations fostered by his relationships with teachers and his parents and bolstered by school-based praise. In terms of the project as a whole, the example of Brad reveals the ways in which children's musical identities are distinctive, formed within certain niches that can foster specific characteristics. These niches, filtering children's experiences through relationships with significant adults, can counteract society-wide trends such as, in Brad's case, a general trend for boys to be reluctant singers.

As also noted in the introduction, we invited child participants to make their own choice of song and this carried important messages for the children in terms of their identity. Songs and song-singing help to affirm allegiances to certain social groups. Charlie in the UK chose one song that was written and performed on a CD by her father. Other children also chose songs that affirmed close family connections and the strong influence of family and national identity on their musical preferences and tastes. Giovanna in Brazil, whose musical tastes were modeled on her father's, liked the song "A Hard Nut to Crack." Michael in Kenya sang "Mary Had a Little Lamb" and "Jesus Loves Me, This I Know," revealing the strong religious identity that has shaped much of his musical experiences and choices. Sissi in Israel sang "Chanukah, Chanukah, Yemey hachanuka," reinforcing the idea that national traditions play a central role in children's identity-formation, with song as a form of expression becoming a channel of expressing these identities. The lyrics of the songs may also reinforce gender identifications. Maiara sang "Feliz da primavera" (in English, "Happy from spring"—see Figure 3.2), a song with stereotypically feminine characteristics, about flowers, and also sang "Butterfly," while Rose in the United States sang "There are Sunny Days in October." These song lyrics also affirm culture-wide, idealized, and somewhat nostalgic conceptions of contemporary childhood as being happy, close to nature, and free from burdens.

Gender in Musical Preference and Musical Engagement

It has long been recognized that adolescent and young adult boys and girls have different musical preferences (Colley, 2008; Green, 1997; Hall, 2005). Although referring to young people older than the children in our study, this work can suggest some ways for conceptualizing musical preferences among younger children in relation to gender differences. After reviewing a series of studies, North and Hargreaves (2008) arrived at the proposition that in general terms, females prefer "softer" musical styles, such as pop, whereas males prefer "harder" musical styles, such as rock. However, according to the authors, it is likely that a correct interpretation points to gender differences concerning the use of music. A study by North, Hargreaves, and O'Neill (2000) conducted with adolescents concluded that the reasons boys and girls listen to certain music styles are different. Boy participants indicated that they use the music they listen to in a process of impression management, to be viewed positively and even to please their group of friends. On the other hand, girls seem to use music for mood optimization, such as when they are going through difficulties or even expressing their feelings or emotional needs.

In talking about the music that they listen to, enjoy, and prefer, often as part of the "show and tell" in which they presented CDs from their own and family collections, the children were again engaged in "identity work." They knew that the musical choices conveyed important messages for defining their musical identities. Although the conclusions of studies were not entirely consistent, there is some evidence to suggest that very young children prefer music on the basis of its general auditory characteristics—loud and fast music being preferred (Lamont, 2002). As children gradually learn the delineated meanings of different styles and genres of music (Green, 1997), their preferences may be more affected by the social meanings the music carries. Studies of adolescent boys and girls suggest that they form preferences for certain types of music for the badge of identity and allegiance to certain groups that music can bestow (Tarrant, North, and Hargreaves, 2002). Where seven-year-olds stand in relation to preferences on grounds of inherent or delineated meanings is difficult to assess. But since pop music was the most preferred style and, in almost all cases, the child's favorite musician was a popular artist, regardless of gender, ethnicity, or religion, we propose that the children in "our" study were already very aware of the subtleties of delineated meanings and they formed their preferences accordingly.

Interestingly, most of "our" female children admire male popular artists. The only exception is Anna, the Italian girl, whose favorite artist is Lady Gaga. Melina in Greece enjoys listening to Greek pop music. Her favorite musician is a young male singer. Maiara in Brazil likes Taiguara, an Uruguayan male singer and composer living in Brazil. Interestingly, the Dutch boy in the project likes a female singer, Celine Dion. Millar (2008) conducted a study on the music preferences of young adults (first-year university students), comprising fifty males and fifty females with a mean age of 19.7 years. Findings indicated that most female participants preferred listening to male pop artists. The author posits that societal valuation of male roles as being superior to female roles causes females to attempt to raise their status by identifying with males. If this were the case in our situation, we would still need to explain why Basje in the Netherlands would prefer a female singer to a male one, and the Italian girl, a singer of the same gender as hers. We also take note of the age gap between "our" children and Millar's participants, and would therefore hesitate to adopt his proposition wholesale. There is definitely a need to conduct more studies on this issue. Musical taste is therefore influenced by a multiplicity of factors.

Gender differences are revealed not just in terms of preferences for styles and genres of music, but also in how boys and girls speak about their engagement with music. North and Hargreaves (2008) classified studies about preference and musical taste into two groups and in relation to attitudes toward music and uses of music. They suggested that girls have more positive attitudes toward music than boys. Earlier Green (1997) had arrived at a similar view, observing that girls' attitudes toward school and each other as musicians are described as cooperative and conformist, in line with the perceived character of classical music and the playing of orchestral instruments. This image extends to the music in which they are involved, which is subsequently viewed in the same way.

Looking at "our" children in light of these findings, the differences between boys' and girls' attitudes can be inferred from their actions and snippets of their dialogue with the researchers. In the case of Sissi in Israel, a positive attitude toward music is revealed in her willingness to take up and enjoy performing on an instrument chosen by a parent. She has had a passion for the cello since she was five, but goes along with her mother's decision that she study piano when problems arose with the cello tuition. Maiara in Brazil exudes positivity toward music in a number of ways. During the interview, she enthuses about her favorite musician (Taiguara of Uruguay), displaying a wealth of knowledge about the circumstances in which he performs his music: "many of his songs were forbidden during the dictatorship." At home, she likes to play school, and plays at teaching various musical instruments. Giovani in Brazil, on the other hand, prefers playing video games to practicing on his mini keyboard. His reluctance is further reinforced by his admission that his mother asked Santa Claus to give him the musical instruments, yet, "I didn't want them." Throughout the interview, he is reluctant to play any of the instruments when he is requested to. Furthermore, when operating the DVD player, he displays greater interest in operating the machine than in the music to be heard.

Gender and Technology

Our Italian colleague visited both a girl and a boy and made lists of their respective technological items, both those in the home for family use and those belonging specifically to the children. As is mentioned in the concluding chapter of this

Table 4.2. Technological devices found in the homes of Italian children Federico and Anna.

Federico	Anna
4 televisions	2 televisions
1 CD/DVD Player	1 CD/DVD player
1 portable TV	1 video recorder
1 desktop computer	1 laptop computer
1 stereo	1 stereo
1 iPod	1 portable CD player
3 mobile phones	2 mobile phones
1 cordless telephone	1 cordless telephone
2 computer toys	2 computer toys
Nintendo	Nintendo
Wii Fit	Interactive kids' DVD
Karaballa musical carpet (musical toy)	Magic wand-tot "winx" (musical toy)

book, we are writing about this project a few years after having visited the children and this home-based technology is thus already out of date. For example, touch-screen pads are now more in use, replacing the large, static computers that were present then in some homes. One of the current challenges of writing about children's everyday music is that the technology and commerce moves forward at a quicker pace than academic research and publishing. Table 4.2 displays the technological devices in the homes of the Italian participants at the time of the study.

Music is embedded in and inseparable from many forms of digitized activities. Brad in the United States enjoys visiting a mall on weekends to play Wii games, at which he is very proficient. Giovani in Brazil prefers playing a video game to playing a musical instrument. His request to Santa Claus is for a race-track. He also plays video games on his grandmother's computer.

In terms of gender differences Comber, Hargreaves, and Colley (1993) suggest that boys are not only more confident in using music technology than girls, but that they also show more interest in music if that music has any connection with technology. In general, the girls in the project tended to view technological devices from a more functional perspective. Maria, the Spanish girl, always had the radio on at home, and had one of her favorite CDs in the car. Rose in the United States seemed to have little interest in computer games, and had no favorite CD. Annie's father, who worked in a flat screen TV industry, had bought her many gadgets, including a computer, but he "does not allow her to use the internet." He bought her educational programs. She also had a DS, a Wii, and a projector. Her father played computer games with her on weekends. She appeared to display competence in the use of the technological devices she had. In her case, male modeling appeared to play a considerable role in her dexterity with the devices. In the case of Michael (the Kenyan boy), while there were various devices such as a radio, CD player, TV, and DVD player in his home, they were either in his parents' room or the guest room. Their location was deliberate, in order to ensure they were used at appropriate times, generally on Friday evenings and on weekends.

Conclusions

As we have emphasized elsewhere in this book, the musical activities that children participate in at home are quite different in nature from out-of-home activities in which they participate at school, on the playground, or in places such as religious settings. Yet most of the understandings of children's acquisition of gender identities in music have arisen from studies of children in school and participating in educational activities. Providing insights into musical activities in the home and showing how other family members, particularly parents, influence those activities, enables us to gain a different perspective on how children build a sense of being a musical boy or girl. What particularly struck us is the importance of parents as role models who can reinforce prevailing cultural stereotypes or help to counter them by providing alternatives. Parents might model alternative musical models, or provide support or encouragement to children to pursue nontypical pathways. At the age of seven children seemed to be balanced between family influence and peer/media influences, with parents still strongly influencing their children's choices and activities. At the same time, however, the influence of peers and the messages from media items, both of which pull children toward conformity to gender norms, hovered in the homes. Children carefully negotiated among these various sources, and their often competing messages, in making their musical decisions and actively fashioning their musical identities.

5 Nurturing MyMUSICal Child

Parental Perspectives and Influences

Theano Koutsoupidou

The roots of music education and development lie in the very beginning of one's life. Prenatal music as a means of the formation of musical tastes, preferences, attitudes, and practices is increasingly acknowledged in research that establishes links between prenatal and postnatal life (e.g., Parncutt, 2009). Children's initial musical experiences play a substantial role in their later musical behaviors. Children are recipients of many stimuli: parents, siblings, school, social and cultural networks become valuable sources of music knowledge, practice, and satisfaction. Musical experience and knowledge can be gained through everyday home activities, spontaneously or with some form of guidance, in the playground or in a school setting. The latter becomes the case for children mostly when entering primary school at the age of five or six years. The music lesson then gradually shifts from being free and play-like to gaining shape and having components of formality.

Children's lives during the years of formal schooling are divided into two main parts—school life and family life—and both environments have the potential to provide motivation to the developing child (Howe and Sloboda, 1991; Sichivitsa, 2007). School life refers mainly to the child's formal schooling and can vary from being educated to making friends, playing, sharing, and in general developing the qualities of a social being. Family life includes the child and the parents, or parents and siblings when applicable. However, grandparents and other relatives or carers are certainly considered to be vital parts of what is called "family" because they are part of a child's everyday home activities and routines. At the young ages of primary school the family is also responsible for the child's social development. Experiences gained together with the family, such as visiting friends, attending various events, visiting playgrounds, going shopping, taking excursions and trips, and so forth, contribute to the child's gradual development of social skills.

In charge of their children's daily schedules, parents usually make decisions regarding what is best for the child to do when at home. Parents make decisions about whether the child should take classes outside of school and which ones would be best. When it comes to music, the parents make decisions regarding the best musical instrument to learn or the best music genre to listen to. Although parents' influence on musical genre preferences tends to fade in the later years of primary school, it is still evident in the early years. Parents' aspirations may also influence their practices regarding their children's experiences in music (McPherson, 2009). They decide which musical materials and resources will be provided to the child, and thus play a substantial role in forming and guiding children's musical experiences. The present chapter examines the role of parents in supervising, guiding, encouraging, or even, perhaps, stifling their children's musical expression and experiences.

Parental Involvement in Music Education

Parents become increasingly involved in the education and well-being of their children in terms of school attendance, academic achievement, and nonschool-based activities. The latter includes helping with school preparation (i.e., homework), out-of-school classes (e.g., music, art, and sports), and leisure activities. A survey of the Department for Children, Schools and Families in England (Peters, Seeds, Goldstein, and Coleman, 2008) reports a major increase of parental involvement in their child's school life compared to previous years. Perhaps more important is the conclusion that "while involvement with homework and school-based activities show little change, parents are now more likely to take part in wider activities, such as reading, cooking, making things and playing sport" (Peters et al., 2008, p. 101).

Different forms of parental involvement have also been investigated, drawing specific frameworks through which family and school communication are promoted (Epstein, 2001). Literature on children's musical development verifies the importance of parental involvement for children's engagement in specific music activities, from free musical play (Berger and Cooper, 2003) to learning a musical instrument (Creech and Hallam, 2003; Davidson, Howe, Moore, and Sloboda, 1996; Zdzinski, 1996). Davidson and colleagues (1996) suggest that the level of mastery in playing a musical instrument depends on the level of parental support during the learning process, and Creech and Hallam (2003) link effective music learning to effective parenting. Parental involvement in a child's music education creates a bond between the child, the parent, and the teachers and this triadic schema becomes beneficial for the child's progress both psychologically and educationally (Creech and Hallam, 2003; McPherson, 2009).

Several researchers address the issue of parental involvement in children's music education as being beneficial both for the actual learning and for building effective relationships and communication between the child and the parents (Berger and Cooper, 2003; de Grätzer, 1999). Through this strong relationship and along with children's need to feel competent, autonomous, and purposeful, most parents help their little ones develop positive attitudes for activities in which they engage and eventually achieve their goals (McPherson, 2009). At the level of higher education, parental support can positively influence students' self-concepts in music (Sichivitsa, 2007), that is, "students' perceptions of their own musical ability and of other adults' opinions of students' musical ability" (Sichivitsa, 2007, p. 59).

The level and nature of parental involvement directly influences children's musical experiences. Parental involvement based on understanding, cooperation, and allowing a certain degree of freedom to the child learner is more likely to have positive outcomes to his or her intrinsic motivation and academic achievement. Children, especially in the early years, need a safe and free environment where musical play eventually transforms to learning. In other words, parental involvement can become critical for a child's musical expression. Berger and Cooper (2003) argue that "certain behaviors of adults and children—such as physical proximity and adult corrections or criticism—extinguished children's free musical play" (p. 162). In a similar way, children's creative potential in music may be nurtured or stifled according to the opportunities they are given by adults (Koutsoupidou, 2008; Koutsoupidou and Hargreaves, 2009; McPherson, 2009).

According to a study by Bradley, Corwyn, Pipes McAdoo, and Garcia Coll (2001), parental involvement may differ according to ethnic and cultural factors. The study, which was carried out in the United States, draws the conclusion that ethnicity and socioeconomic status are linked with the likelihood of children's being exposed to certain experiences at home. Moreover, according to the same study, low income can become a major stress factor that potentially leads to parents' lack of communication and physical affection toward their children. Mayer (2002) supports the above-mentioned arguments, suggesting that "the effect of parental income is positive for all outcomes" and that "there is some evidence to suggest that income is more important during early childhood for schooling outcomes" (p. 66). These outcomes, as reported by Mayer (2002), include enhanced cognitive test scores, socioemotional well-being, mental health, fewer behavior problems, higher measures of health, teenage childbearing, educational outcomes, and future economic status.

To summarize, the literature on children's musical development demonstrates that parents can play an important role in forming their children's musical experiences and suggests links between effective music learning and effective parenting as well as between parental involvement and sociocultural factors.

Design and Scope

A large body of previous studies has adopted research methodologies based on "cause–effect" schemas, focusing on different effects, such as effective learning and academic achievement (e.g., Creech and Hallam, 2003; Zdzinski, 1996). The present chapter continues the discussion of parental influences, in an effort to emphasize music education issues that are linked to parental perspectives and influences. These include reasons that children initially engage with certain music activities and the factors that influence their maintenance in these activities. The aim is to gain a better comprehension of children's musical development and the factors that affect the construction of their musical identities through a combination of formal and informal learning (Folkestad, 2006), and school and home activities that cover all aspects of music experience, including music listening, singing, instrument playing, moving and dancing, reading music, improvising, and composing.

This chapter is based on interviews with children in six different families and their parents ($n=12$). Four families were based in Greece (Nafpaktos), Israel (Misgav), Kenya (Nairobi), and Taiwan (Taipei), respectively, and two in the United States (Texas). As discussed in chapters 1 and 2 (this volume), data were collected by different researchers (in this case five) and in some cases assistants were employed to aid practical issues such as videotaping. The interviews, although based on a general common project protocol, were unstructured and focused on the everyday musical activities of each child both at school and at home and in relation to various family routines and preferences. Although the data provided an international perspective, this study does not seek to draw conclusions by generalizing certain musical practices as strictly related to their geographical contexts, nor does it aim to make comparisons between countries and/or continents. Still, some comparisons are worthy of discussion as they shed light on the data. According to Tudge (2008), "explicit comparisons are helpful in that they can inform us about the different values, beliefs, and practices of different groups, and can make explicit the historical, cultural, or social reasons for those different values, beliefs, and practices" (p. 87).

Conversations with parents as well as some parental interventions during the interviews with the children revealed a variety of themes that could be relevant to nurturing children's musical worlds. These themes include parents' musical backgrounds and personal experiences in relation to music, their own dreams and aspirations regarding their children's musical futures, their musical tastes and routines, for example, religious music practices or attendance at certain performances. Moreover, the issue of financial restrictions that may affect children's involvement in musical activities was raised, as well as the parents' general appreciation of music together with the sociocultural factors that may influence their attitudes toward music and music education.

Nurturing MyMUSICal Child

Backgrounds and Aspirations

Current societies portray shifts and new trends compared to previous decades in terms of educational opportunities. These eventually affect new generations of parents who are usually well-educated and sufficiently informed about their children's needs. Parents seek their children's well-being through a thorough education that will positively affect their general development. The arts—and music in particular—are among the aspects that form the scheme of a quality education. The latter might occur as a result of some parents' efforts to fulfill personal gaps created by what was lacking in their own education.

Parents express that they are prepared to offer their children the full potential to study music and gain experiences that they never had the chance to gain. Their own aspirations, though, can sometimes lead to certain music choices, such as musical styles or instrument preferences, guided by their own personal tastes. Michael's mother in Kenya articulates her expectations regarding her son's involvement in music activities:

> I didn't have that opportunity myself, and I always admired people who can do much more than just what the regular system can offer, that they can see whether they are talented and train . . . so that is something that I've always longed for. I would give my children an opportunity to do that as much as I am able to. And that goes also for art, drama, . . . so that they can express their talents. If you are able to give them that exposure, it is good to give them. Being a professional musician, I don't think I would go there; but being able to be comfortable with the piano, play the guitar . . . that is something that I think is good to do.

Rose's mother in the United States also links her daughter's musical experiences to her own dreams and personal educational gaps. However, she does not place rigid restrictions on her child's musical experiences, and allows herself to observe Rose in order to draw conclusions about her child's areas of excellence and interests:

> I'd like to see her play the piano because I always wanted to and never did. I don't want to push her, but I would like to encourage her to do it. Because I think she has a gift and she memorizes quickly and well. And a lot of times when I see her singing with her friends she's leading the song and her friends are humming along. So I do notice things like that.

Sissi's mother in Israel is another example of parents guiding their child's musical experiences. She makes her own selection of instrument—the piano—according to her personal beliefs about the right way for Sissi to begin her music instruction. However, the same mother had initially given her daughter the option to choose her instrument. She revealed her own aspirations only after her daughter's choice did not work out.

> At age five she decided she wanted the cello. . . . So we brought her to [teacher's name], who's considered overall the master of the cello and . . . it didn't work out. He's excellent with older [pupils], but with younger ones, he doesn't know what to do with them . . . I looked for a teacher, not an instrument. We went at it all backwards. This is essentially how we arrived at the piano, not because she said "I want the piano" . . . I told myself that we'll go with an instrument for which the teacher's good and overall it's an instrument that gives a good grounding. If afterwards she'll want to go for something else she'll go for something else. That's the agreement.

Sissi's mother raises another issue in music education: the influence of the music teacher, which recalls Creech's (2009) findings about more or less effective "teacher–pupil–parent triads." Being a music teacher herself, the Israeli mother makes clear what her expectations are: "[Sissi] has . . . she knows that Mom equals music; she knows that from all the daughters in the house she's the closest to Mom's dream." The parent's "dream" often becomes a vital factor that guides a child's music instruction at early ages. The effect of this form of parental pressure can have positive or negative outcomes depending on its level and nature. Taking the form of parental support, guidance, and encouragement, parents' aspirations can benefit the child's better learning. However, parental aspirations and dreams can also have opposite results. Extreme pressure, both psychologically and practically, through music practice can create negative attitudes toward music and counteract effective music learning. In such cases, children might develop negative feelings about music and as a result might withdraw from music classes and other activities.

Various beliefs linked to cultural and religious issues can also influence parental aspirations regarding their children's education. In many cultures, music practice is directly related to religion via religious activities that include solo or choir singing and instrument playing for purposes of prayer. Parents' aspirations in such cases are designed to serve these purposes. For example, one parent said: "As a Christian I would like him to use his gifts for the glory of God. So if he ever chooses to develop music into a career, I would pray that he does it in church because of our faith. But again, matters of faith you cannot legislate; you can wish, but you can leave it to God, so you never know."

Benefits of Music

Interestingly, parental levels of music knowledge do not seem to affect their attitudes toward their children's music education. Among a total of twelve participating parents, only four report being formally educated in music. However, all parents interviewed for the study express their appreciation of the benefits of music as a means of expression, relaxation, therapy, and entertainment. Boyd's mother in the United States stresses the therapeutic effect of music: "Music is such good therapy when I hear it and I want him to experience that too." Annie's mother in Taiwan emphasizes the social perspective of music engagement and learning. She finds it important to help her daughter develop a hobby so that she can enjoy music, not only for the sake of music itself but also for its socializing aspects: "My husband and I feel that cello lessons will probably help her concentration, so she could be more focused. Also, it could cultivate her to be music literate. So when she is older[,] other than karaoke and movies she would also go to pop concerts or classical music concerts with friends. I feel this has to do with a hobby that you foster when you are young."

For some parents music education is not strictly about learning music and how to play a musical instrument. They consider it important for both children and adults to comprehend and value the positive effects of music on their mental and psychological wellbeing. Having no formal training Michael's father in Kenya points out the importance of musical appreciation: "Not everyone must be a musician; we also need people who are good at listening and appreciating, and I do appreciate music seriously, and I wish I could play, but I can't play." Michael's mother, also a supporter of musical appreciation, continues:

> I would like him to learn music, because I find him tending to just play on the piano, the drums, which I think is a good thing, but I would like him to have the discipline to learn music. I wouldn't force him if he didn't quite want to, in the future, to be a musician or whatever. But I would like him to appreciate music. So that it is not just noise, it is not just . . . there is rhythm . . . it is properly played.

Socioeconomic Factors

Music learning requires involvement in different types of informal and formal experiences (Folkestad, 2006). Informal music activities include, for example, casual music listening at home or in the car with music styles usually being chosen by a parent; experimenting with sound-producing objects such as kitchen utensils and toys; and singing learned or improvised songs alone or together with a sibling or a parent. Formal experiences, in turn, are gained through extracurricular activities such as noncurriculum and out-of-school classes, group or one-to-one music lessons in instruments, voice, or dance, and attendance at music events. The extent of music provision available to a child depends on the parents' personal appreciation of the benefits of music and music education as well as on socioeconomic factors.

Certain societies value music significantly more than others, which means that parents more eagerly encourage their children's engagement in formal music activities. Likewise, some educational systems place music higher or lower in the school curriculum in terms of necessity.[1] These differences are not inevitably linked to the economic status of a state or local area. Wealthier families can certainly overcome any financial obstacles involved in providing music materials and technological devices that potentially aid music engagement. This, however, is not sufficient when the same parents do not value music or do not get actively involved in their children's musical experiences. The data analysis revealed that informal, casual music experiences are more likely to take place within families that express a high appreciation for music and music education whether or not they can afford the extra expenses entailed.

When discussing the financial capacity for providing music materials, one should essentially refer to the substantial cost to a family's budget when it comes to formal music experiences. This could become a prohibitive factor in music class attendance when parents map their children's education. The socioeconomic background of the families involved in this study indicates that financial issues indeed became an obstacle for their choices regarding their children's music education in the long term.

Michael's father expresses concern about his son's progress in music due to the large financial demands associated with learning a musical instrument. He believes that large financial demands are often an obstacle to a child's attendance of music classes, making particular reference to the extraordinary costs of buying a good quality instrument and taking private instrumental lessons. Michael enjoys playing the drums and the piano. His ability seems very promising in terms of further developing his music abilities, but according to his father, this may become difficult if the family cannot afford the expense:

> I would like to buy a serious drum. It is very costly, so I have been mark timing about it. I'd like to also probably take him [his son] to a place where he could learn drums more formally. So yes, we'd like to develop him. . . . It is unfortunate that I find music so expensive. Whether you are talking about instruments, or the lessons, it is prohibitive, especially the lessons. Every session [costs] so much money. That I find unfortunate. Sometimes you have to really look around before you find anybody who would be willing to work within your budget. . . . I'd like to have a whole library of musical instruments for them [his children]. Sometimes we [parents] are not able to buy as we would want to; it is like you really have to budget before you get one.

Accessibility to music events is another factor that determines the extent of music provision available for a child. Attendance at music concerts, festivals, and so on can become problematic when family financial restrictions occur. Moreover, issues of geographical proximity and availability of quality music events arise when families are situated in rural areas. In countries with inadequate regional development, major cultural events tend to take place in only two or three city centers in which the largest percentages of the country's population reside. This was clearly voiced by Melina's mother in Greece and Annie's mother in Taiwan:

> I can't live without music . . . I listen to everything. It depends on my mood. I also like going to live concerts. But you can hardly find them here. I usually go to Patra [a nearby city]. Many Greek singers give concerts there in the summer.

> In Taiwan, sometimes the facilities are not that good. Most of the shows take place in Taipei Arena, but the Taipei Arena is not very good.

Learning Support

The review of the literature presented earlier stressed the importance of parental support to facilitate better musical understanding, appreciation, and learning. Parental support can take different forms, from psychological support to active participation in studying and practicing music. In extreme cases, support may turn into pressure that eventually stifles a child's music interest. Parental involvement in their children's musical play not only influences the child's motivation but also strengthens the communication between the parent and the child (de Grätzer, 1999), while the level and means of support can vary according to parents' cultural values (García-Coll et al., 2002).

Some parents consider "being there" as vital for a child's musical progress when studying music formally. Data from interviews with parents and children revealed three different levels of "being there" during their children's music practice at home:

- Just listening, sometimes while doing some other housework;
- Simply attending the music practice sessions, but without offering verbal comments or feedback;
- Actively attending the music practice sessions, by making comments and giving feedback.

Each of the above categories of parental participation is represented, respectively, in the following quotations by Annie's mother, Michael's father, and Sissi's mother:

> My mom is usually cooking when I practice tap dancing, but she listens to me practicing cello. [parent just listening]

> Every time I hear him on the piano I ask him "is that what you have learnt?" I can't tell whether he is playing well or not because I am not a music person, but I keep hoping that as I insist he will see that I am interested and hopefully play well. [parent just attending]

> But music that she really, really gets into, those are pieces that I had something about, I had a story about them, and with a little mediating [on my part] she was already into it, and then the music became hers. [parent actively attending]

However, not all family activities are related to formal learning. Parents also make up music with their children spontaneously with no specific learning goals, mostly for fun, as seen in the conversation of Rose's parents:

FATHER: I make up a lot of songs with her.

MOTHER: We're not really good at it.

FATHER: But I am.

MOTHER: I just hum at church because I don't want to offend those around me.

FATHER: But I sing really well in the shower.

Similarly, other people involved in the task of childrearing, such as grandparents in the case of Melina in Greece, may enjoy musical interactions with the child. Although the discussion in this chapter focuses on parental influences, other caregivers who spend a significant amount of time with a child are also considered to play an important role in their music development:

MOTHER: Why don't you sing to us the song that you and your grandpa sing together Melina?

MELINA: No, I don't want to [she gets a bit shy].

MOTHER: Ok, I'll sing it then [she starts singing a Greek traditional song].

[Melina starts laughing.]

MOTHER: They often sing together with her grandpa. Her grandpa is a great dancer, too!

INTERVIEWER: Do you spend lots of time with your grandparents?

MELINA: Yes, I go to their house, we eat together . . .

Support of learning can lead to parental pressure, as illustrated in the following quotation from the interview held in Israel. The mother, although acknowledging that maybe she does not follow the correct approach, keeps forcing her daughter to attend activities that she is not very enthusiastic about:

INTERVIEWER: Who suggested to you to go to the choir? Your mom?

SISSI: Mommy made me go.

INTERVIEWER: Your mom made you go? And you don't like it so much? Does it cause you suffering?

SISSI: [indicates an affirmative response].

INTERVIEWER: A whole lot?

SISSI: Also.

MOTHER: She really loves the songs of the choir. She simply told you that she doesn't want this choir. . . . Every lesson after choir rehearsal she sits and sings all the songs one after another—and every time she tells me "I don't want to go." Something I haven't succeeded to track down, for example, is what's the real reason she doesn't want to [go to choir rehearsals].

Later in the interview, the mother added:

MOTHER: I think that this is the dilemma: how much, if any, [to put] pressure on studying music, since this is clear to me that it's necessary; there's no doubt, and afterwards how much actually to put an emphasis on practicing. I think that here, this was the question.

Conclusions

The aim of this chapter was to raise issues of music education linked to parental perspectives and influences. These issues included the reasons that children initially engaged with certain music activities and the factors that influenced their maintenance in these activities. These were investigated through their parents' backgrounds and aspirations, learning support, and provision available in each case. As stated earlier in the chapter, although the data provided an international perspective, the aim of this study was not to generalize certain musical practices as strictly related to their geographical contexts.

What is evident from the interview data is that parents certainly have the potential to enhance their children's motivation in order to both initiate and sustain their interest in a music education path. However, their choices and decisions are frequently forced by their personal educational gaps that transform to aspirations for their own children's futures; in such cases, certain limitations occur in children's music education that may come into contrast with their personal wills. Sustaining interest in certain music activities may also be determined by socioeconomic as well as geographical factors, such as proximity to cultural centers and events.

Nurturing a musical child is the result of a combination of factors that include people, places, environments, and policies. Parental roles can be critical for a child's music life and education. It can be argued that the most encouraging finding of this study is the high levels of appreciation that parents express for music and music education, regardless of geographical, social, or educational criteria. The quotation that follows indeed presents one example of a shift from disregard or ignorance about music that may have been present in the past toward the value and appreciation of today. At the same time, it expresses a spirit of hope and positivism for the days to come in music education. As the father in Kenya stated:

> I think they [the children nowadays] are luckier in the sense that one can, for example, have a piano in the house at this age, for us that was . . . you don't go there. You only see it in church. And our parents would not even allow us to play music per se, because, number one, it was not in the curriculum, number two it was viewed like more of a waste of time, and where is it going to take you, so why bother. So, if anyone in our generation learned music it is simply because it was in their blood. They were just talented and they had to do it, but not because it was nurtured. There was hardly any nurturing. So they [the children nowadays] have an opportunity because we are able to identify a talent and we are able to invest in it. Then I guess they would probably turn out better than us.

Note

1. Necessity in this context means appreciating and valuing music, which is demonstrated in the amount of hours devoted to it in the curriculum.

6 Middle-Class Musical Childhoods

Autonomy, Concerted Cultivation, and Consumer Culture

Beatriz Ilari

Social class is one of several important markers of childhood socialization as it directly impacts how children interact with family members, peers, and teachers, in a wide range of social groups and institutions (Kaufman, 2005; Lareau, 2010). In the past few decades, a considerable body of work on social inequality, social mobility, and status attainment has emerged, particularly in the field of sociology. Regarding social mobility, an area that has received much attention pertains to the reproduction of social-class standing from one generation to the next (Kaufman, 2005). Important works, such as Bourdieu's (1984) analysis of the hierarchies of taste discussed in the well-known book *Distinction*, for example, have attempted to explain the complexities involved in social mobility, claiming that social-class standing is quite entrenched and difficult to change (Kaufman, 2005).

Interestingly, only in recent years have issues of social-class standing begun to gain attention from music education researchers (e.g., Bates, 2012; Wright, 2010). Likewise, theories of social reproduction (e.g., Lareau, 2011) are yet to be fully embraced by scholars in the field. Until fairly recently, most studies in music education have treated social class as an independent variable, as is often the case in psychological research, with the vast majority focusing on students from North America and West European countries. Even if participants in these studies normally came from the middle class, there was little discussion concerning how the latter was defined or how specific musical practices related to the reproduction of social class standing across generations.

By contrast, in the field of sociology, studies on social class reproduction have typically focused on the working class, with comparatively less attention devoted to the middle class (Kaufman, 2005). This appears to be the case where young children are concerned (Tudge, 2008). If it is true that middle-class status is not only structurally determined, but also an active, constructed, and negotiated process (see Kaufman, 2005; Lareau, 2011), then it is central to understand some of its contributing factors.

One way for families to transmit social status to their children is through cultural capital, or the ability to appreciate, decode, and understand "high" arts such as literature, visual arts, and classical music, to name a few (Bourdieu, 1984). For Bourdieu, music is a classificatory practice, and this is illustrated using the example of classical music, which is more commonly associated with the high class. Bourdieu's theory is not without its criticisms, of course, including the notion that we live in postmodern times, when distinctions between high and popular culture are gradually becoming less well-defined and more complex (see Buckingham, 2011; Vincent and Ball, 2007). But arguably, even in postmodern days, middle-class families still attempt to maintain the status quo, by doing what they feel will grant their children some advantages later in life. This might include enrolling children in formal programs in music and the visual arts, constantly exposing them to arts organizations such as theaters and museums, or through multiple forms of collecting art (Banks, 2011).

As I will argue throughout this chapter, there is a tacit and fairly loose notion of a middle-class musical childhood that dominates the lives of urban parents and their children in some parts of the world, which can be viewed as an important factor in social class reproduction. That is, musical experiences, in and out of schools, as well as participation in formal music instruction and consumption of specific repertoires, instruments, musical toys, digital music, and technological gadgets help to construct a particular view of musical childhood (see Young, chapter 1, this volume) that is directly associated with the middle class. This chapter, then, examines the construction of middle-class musical childhoods in the discourses and musical practices of children and parents who took part in the MyPlace MyMusic research project.

Notes on Data Interpretation: Middle Class, the Local, and the Global

Before delving more deeply into the actual data, it is important to acknowledge that middle class is a complex construct that has been defined in a multitude of ways and in accordance with different levels of economic development in individual countries (Ravallion, 2010). For example, in the Western-dominated educational and psychological literature, the concept of middle class has typically been constructed through combinations of parental education (e.g., holding a college degree), occupation (e.g., working in semiprofessional, professional, or managerial occupations), and income (e.g., Banks, 2011; Hollingshead, 1975; Kaufman, 2005). Yet these variables are obviously susceptible to local issues such as values and affordances in different parts of the world, including access to education, wages, and economic issues, to name a few. Therefore, it seems obvious that while all participating children in the current study came from middle-class families as locally articulated, there certainly were differences among them (Ilari, 2013a; Young, 2012b). For this reason, each individual research team member, who was a university professor (or a doctoral student) and came from the middle class, as locally articulated, was left to find one or two study participants who came from a socioeconomic background similar to their own (for more information on the methodology, refer to chapters 1 and 2). Therefore, when speaking of the middle class throughout the chapter, I rely on these locally constructed notions, which are fairly loose and culturally bound. Also, because social class is not a stand-alone characteristic, but is often linked to other markers of socialization and social identity, such as culture, ethnicity, race, religious beliefs, and lifestyles, these were also taken into account during the analysis and interpretation of data.

In addition, rather than taking a strictly comparative approach, which is typical of much cross-cultural research, my main goal was to understand how social class (i.e., middle class) affected children's everyday musical engagement. Without the intent of making overarching generalizations, I was curious to know how middle-class families in different parts of the world perceived, valued, and engaged in music. I also wanted to know whether current theories of middle-class family values and practice would apply to a small yet diverse sample. To address these questions, three important and interrelated aspects that are said to be central to middle-class family life were used as main theoretical lenses in the analysis of children's musical engagement (see Figure 6.1), namely, parental beliefs regarding children's autonomy and self-direction (Kohn, 1963, 1995), concerted cultivation (Lareau, 2011), and participation in consumer culture (Buckingham, 2011; Pugh, 2009). Because these three aspects stem from research conducted predominantly in North American and West European contexts, it was also important to carefully consider both global and local issues (Schousboue, 2005), as they related to children's musical engagement. As will be seen, while there were some similarities among study participants, local issues such as varied conceptions of child and cultural values were also seen to influence how families perceived and engaged with music in everyday life.

Nurturing Children's Autonomy, Self-Direction, and Choice in Music

Middle-class families with children are said to exhibit some particular beliefs, values, and practices. Based on data collected in different parts of the world (predominantly Western countries), Kohn (1963, 1995) suggested that middle-class parents, defined as those with more education and working in professional areas, are more likely to explain their own successes on the basis of autonomy and self-direction. By contrast, working-class parents, or those with lower levels of education and working in the nonprofessional arena (e.g., services), tend to correlate

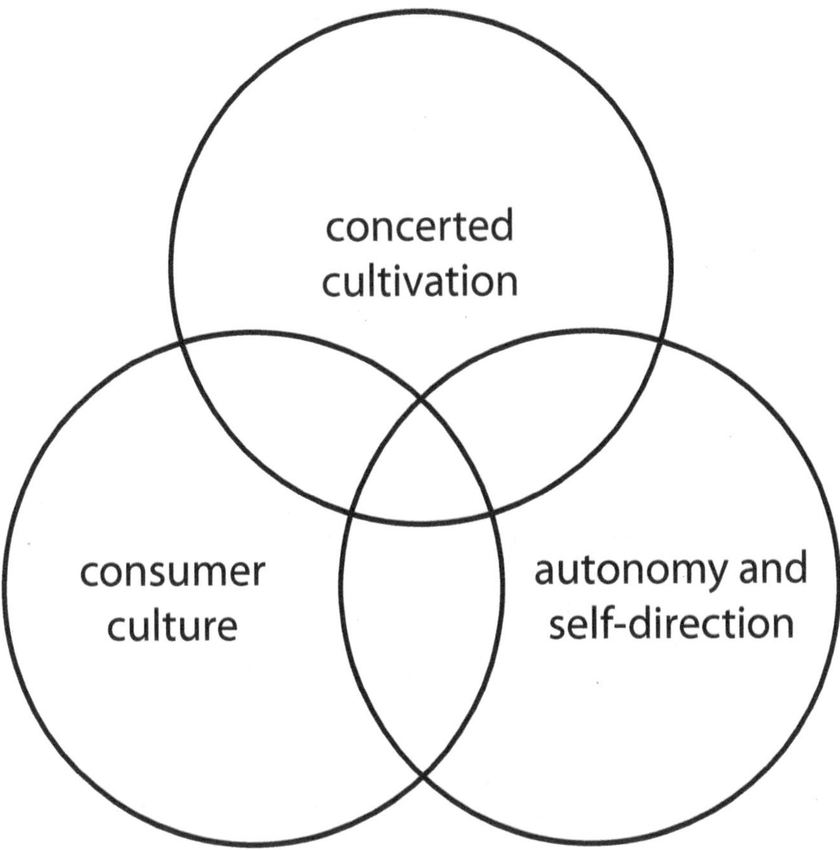

Figure 6.1. Three aspects of middle-class family life and parenting.

their own successes with the ability to follow rules created by others. These opposing views are likely to influence how middle- and working-class parents raise their children (see Tudge et al., 2013).

As regards musical parenting, or the set of beliefs, values, and behaviors that parents have and engage in with their children concerning music (Ilari, Moura, and Bourscheidt, 2011), it was possible to see how autonomy, self-direction, and choice were valued and exercised across participating families. Based on a combination of values regarding music learning and of observations of children's musical inclinations and interests in everyday life, parents reinforced their own notions of autonomy, self-direction, and musical choice for their children. Interestingly, and perhaps unsurprisingly, in most cases, parents spoke about learning musical formally as an opportunity for children to make choices, and this was particularly true when formal music learning was still hypothetical. The Kenyan father, for example, spoke about his musical wishes for his son, but not without stressing the fact that there would be no "forcing" of any kind:

> I would like him to learn music, because I find him tending to just play on the piano, the drums, which I think is a good thing, but I would like him to have the discipline to learn music. I wouldn't force him if he didn't quite want to, in the future, to be a musician or whatever. But I would like him to appreciate music. So that it is not just noise, it is not just . . . there is rhythm . . . it is properly played.

Likewise, a US mother stated that she would like to see her daughter play the piano because she never had such an opportunity growing up. The "choice factor" was also part of her discourse, when she stated that she did not want to "push" but rather "encourage" her child to learn how to play piano (refer to quote in chapter 5, this volume).

Importantly, however, when seven-year-olds were already enrolled in formal music lessons, it became obvious that choice came with some caveats. The Taiwanese mother, for example, described how the selection of an instrument was fully negotiated between child, parents, and teacher:

> We started to think that she needed some quiet, peaceful activities. And she really loved cello. We thought she should start with piano, but she resisted. She said she only wanted to play cello. So, we waited until the teacher said she would be able to hold a cello. She also grew a little taller. So, she started the lessons in the spring semester of kindergarten, or maybe that was the fall semester of the first grade. I think it was the spring semester of kindergarten.

Later in the interview, she explained how she had not given up on the idea of her daughter Annie taking piano lessons, but how she also believed in self-selection if music learning were to be effective. Her argument was based on her own negative experience of being forced to learn the piano in childhood:

> For me, I resisted piano lessons when I was little. Even now I can still recall vividly, the teacher would stand next to me with a stick. If I played the wrong key, she would hit me immediately. If I did not play well, my mother would also punish me. So, I know how bad that feeling could be. After six years of lessons, I told my mother that schoolwork at middle school had become quite burdensome, and I stopped taking the lessons. But I know that kind of feeling. Also, it takes a lot of time to study an instrument. So, we let her take new classes when she wants to. I feel that she will persist in learning a new thing only when she's really interested in it. So, we never ask her, do you want to learn this? Do you want to learn that? This does not only apply to music, but also all other things. If you keep on telling her to do this or to learn that, it's definitely a lose–lose situation.

The Israeli mother, who was a professional musician, also explained how the choice of musical instrument resulted from her daughter's desires and experience with actual teachers. Likewise, one of the Dutch mothers, who sang in a choir for over a decade, discussed at length how the child's desire was taken into account in decisions that involved dropping out of a music program and starting a different one. That is, the child had some degree of choice and autonomy, with the parent serving as mediator but not imposing his or her will. This behavior, as Kohn (1963, 1995) would argue, is more typical of middle-class than working-class parents. Interestingly, in all these cases, parents were referring to learning classical music formally. Along with the high status that is often attributed to formal music education in some parts of the world, particularly the learning of classical music (Bourdieu, 1984), was also related to the transmission of differential advantages to children, even if parents did not seem to be fully aware of this.

Autonomy and choice were more restricted when children were downloading music or selecting songs. Here, parents seemed to hold varied conceptions of children, childhood, and musical appropriateness. Parents often censored repertoires or specific musical practices, even if they were intended or considered suitable for children (see Ilari, 2013a). The Danish and the Greek mothers, for example, explained how they scrutinized the repertoires that their daughters were exposed to through the media and via different forms of digital technology. The Taiwanese mother also expressed her concerns regarding inappropriate, musical and extramusical contents, in this case, as they were associated with the experience of consuming musicals:

RESEARCHER: In terms of providing Annie with music learning experience, in addition to cello lessons, you would take her to almost any shows that she likes? Provided that you think the show is suitable to her.

MOTHER: Yeah. Like earlier, she mentioned *Mamma Mia!*. We thought there was some content that's not suitable for her age. Children nowadays mature too early. So, I told my husband to hold it [off] for now. She did watch the movie [version], which I do regret a little now.

This excerpt suggests that while discourses of autonomy, self-direction, and choice were a constant in parental interviews, parents were still monitoring the repertoires to which their children were being exposed. Such behavior is also consistent with concerted cultivation, or, another aspect of middle-class family life.

Concerted Cultivation and Music Learning in Families across the World

Another important aspect of middle class family life that has received considerable attention from Western scholars is parental engagement in concerted cultivation (Lareau, 2011). Following the logic of cultural capital (Bourdieu, 1984), concerted cultivation relates to participation in a wide range of organized (or extracurricular) activities that will help confer advantages on middle-class children (Lareau, 2011). Organized activities are those that are usually structured, adult-led, and offered for groups of children from the same age group. In addition, organized activities normally focus on the development of specific social, cognitive, or motor skills through playing a musical instrument or participating in a particular sports modality, along with the occupation of children's time in a positive and safe environment (Mahoney, Larson, Eccles, and Lorde 2005).

Participation in organized activities is said to grant middle-class children a sense of entitlement, as they learn to interact with and question adults and institutions, by addressing them as "relative equals" (Lareau, 2010, p. 238). In middle-class families there is also constant dialogue between children and adults, leading children to develop larger vocabularies, greater verbal agility, higher levels of comfort with figures of authority, and greater familiarity with abstract concepts (Lareau, 2010). In other words, middle-class children learn to reason, negotiate, and make compromises with their adult counterparts, which are useful abilities later in life. In some ways, this is also an exercise of autonomy and self-direction, as discussed earlier.

Concerning verbal abilities and children's apparent comfort levels with the interviewers, most children who took part in the MyPlace MyMusic project were outspoken. For example, Giovanna in Brazil and Melina in Greece spoke to the researchers as if they were equals, in the presence of their parents. Yet, some children seemed to be more constrained by their parents' presence: Michael in Kenya and Christine in Singapore appeared to be very shy during certain moments of the interview, constantly looking at their parents in search of affirmation. Field notes shared by the Singaporean researcher express this well:

> The visit was carried out by the researcher with an audio recorder and a video camera in hand. Both father and mother were present during the visit. Christine was shy at the beginning refusing to say very much. She warmed up after 20 minutes and appeared a lot more comfortable as she started to interject her parents' conversation with the researcher and when she was singing and playing the piano. However, when it comes to the "show and tell" section, Christine was once again reluctant to say much and pointed repeatedly to her parents for answers.

While these behaviors may represent profound cultural differences in parenting and cultural codes regarding children's attitudes toward parents, including in regard to compliance (Huang and Lamb, 2015), they may also stem from the novelty of the interview process. Still, a closer examination of data revealed that it was in the intersection between parental beliefs and attitudes that traces of concerted cultivation appeared to be the most prominent (Ilari, 2013a). In this sense, two interrelated aspects were particularly important: parental anxiety about their children's everyday lives, including musical lives (Furedi, 2001), and busy children (Ilari, 2013a).

Some parents showed a high degree of anxiety regarding their own roles in children's musical development and growth. One US mother, for example, expressed how she felt that she was not doing enough to nurture her daughter's musical abilities, although the child appeared to be highly stimulated, musically speaking, in the home from birth, and attended an early childhood music program from babyhood to the preschool years. Likewise, the Spanish mother used the term "obsession" to define her concerns about teaching her child to listen to musical structures in the repertoire that was played at home. Thus, there was some degree of anxiety toward music learning in parental discourses (Furedi, 2001), but it seemed to be more prominent in certain families (e.g., US, Taiwanese) than others (e.g., Brazilian, Greek). It is likely that a combination of parental musical experiences, preferences, and local values associated with musical practices played a role in parental anxieties about music learning.

But no trace of concerted cultivation was greater than the idea of keeping children busy and fully enrolled in a wide range of organized activities—including musical programs—that would eventually help them excel in the future. While all children in the study took part in at least one organized activity—ranging from ceramics (Israeli girl), horseback riding (Brazil), instrumental lessons (Israel, Singapore, Taiwan, United States), sports (Taiwan, Spain, Greece), to scouts club (the Netherlands)—it was the Taiwanese girl who was afforded the greatest number of organized activities. These included private lessons/coaching in cello, tennis, and swimming, different group activities offered after school, such as girl scouts, soccer, cooking, watercolor, Chinese class, actors' workshop, and French. Music learning appeared to be particularly important for this family. Consistent with the rationale of concerted cultivation and with Bourdieu's theories (1984), the Taiwanese mother was eager to state that learning classical music would confer a certain degree of sophistication on her child: "I feel that she should also develop a habit in music. In general, when a person is well versed in music, although this may sound superficial, the person seems to carry more elegance."

While all interviewed parents saw value in enrolling their children in organized activities, family life did not always revolve around them, as in Lareau's (2011) work with middle-class families in the United States. In addition, for some children, like Maiara in Brazil and Basje in the Netherlands, participation in organized musical activities revolved, to some extent, around their parents' interests and work. Maiara tagged along with her parents to capoeira lessons. Basje attended occasional choir rehearsals and performances with his mother. Thus, some traces of concerted cultivation were evident in the data, but appeared much more robust in some families and cultures than in others. This raises the question as to whether concerted cultivation is more a Western phenomenon found in certain countries and cultures, or a universal, middle-class behavior that appears in varied levels, in different families across the world. Underlying the concept of concerted cultivation is the ideology held by many parents that childhood is a period of preparation for adulthood (Kremer-Sadlik and Fatigante, 2015), and that children are a "project" (Lareau, 2011).

Consumer Culture, Musical Consumption, and the Economy of Dignity

Middle-class families are also known to engage in acts of consumption, or the purchase, use, appropriation, and adaptation of commercial goods, both individually and collectively (Buckingham, 2011). As Buckingham (2011) suggested, "contemporary childhoods are lived out in a world of commercial goods and services" (p. 5). While marketing to children is far from new, the ever growing pressure to consume permeates the multiple environments in which children navigate in everyday life—from the home through the media, the school, and the community at large (Young and Ilari, 2012). In times of globalization and constant exchanges, this seems to hold true for the majority of the world as well (Ilari, Moura, and Bourscheidt, 2011).

A closer examination of the MyPlace, MyMusic data revealed some interesting patterns of musical consumption. Musical instruments were a common feature of many households, although numbers and types varied enormously. While instruments of the Western classical tradition such as cellos, violins, and pianos predominated in some families (e.g., in Taiwan, Singapore, Israel, UK, United States), in others, there were more instruments from the local culture such as *berimbaus*, *afoxés* (Brazil), and *trampouline* (Kenya), along with some rather unusual ones, like a nose flute in the Danish home. Musical toys, from singing dolls to more sophisticated electronic devices such as Wii games, digital players, microphones, and iPods were also available in most homes. But the most interesting commonality among families appeared when the contents of musical CDs and DVDs available in the homes were scrutinized. In all families, it was possible to find a combination of CDS and DVDs of children's music (traditional tunes), soundtracks from sitcoms, musicals, Disney films and other movies (e.g., *Barbie and the Diamond Castle*, *High School Musical*, *Shrek*, *The Wizard of Oz*, *Mamma Mia!*), and pop hits by different artists, including renowned pop stars like Lady Gaga and Justin Biber, and local artists like Michalis (Greece), Marisa Monte (Brazil), Anne Linnet (Denmark), and Lucio Dalla and Eros Ramazzotti (Italy). Comparatively speaking, recordings of children's music were more predominant in some households (e.g., United States) than in others (e.g., Brazil), although pop music and soundtracks for movies and musicals were staples of most (if not all) homes. By contrast, classical music recordings appeared mainly in homes where children were learning how to play instruments from this tradition (e.g., in Taiwan and Israel).

This choice of repertoire is interesting because it relates to the existence of a pattern of musical consumption in urban middle classes worldwide in the globalized world. Our data suggest that by age seven, children in different countries are already enculturated into the world of Disney movies and tunes and popular music, and they consume a wide range of toys and gadgets heavily marketed by the corporate world (see Buckingham, 2011; Pugh, 2010). Furthermore, the idea that seven-year-olds in different parts of the world are immersed in the world of popular and commercial music raises questions concerning conceptions of children and childhood in general and in music education, which tends to favor repertoires that are arguably more child-oriented This is far from surprising because the consumption of popular and commercial music is still viewed by many as problematic and even harmful to children's development and well-being. While some consider the lyrics of popular music a major concern (for a discussion, see North and Hargreaves, 2008), others advocate that the consumption of commercial music such as soundtracks and their associated products (e.g., toys, costumes, books) contributes to a massive commodification of childhood (see Buckingham, 2011).

Debates about consumerism, the commodification of childhood and its potential harms abound in current times. Consumerism has typically been viewed as a negative and corruptive force that encourages children to become too materialistic and less focused on what childhood should be, or an "Eden-like space, a source of positive moral and aesthetic values, of 'imagination' and 'innocence' "(Buckingham, 2011, p. 59). Yet, as Buckingham has argued, consumption is also a domain that may include constraint and control, as well as choice and creativity, because it is not an individual act, but one that is embedded in a complex web of social relationships. This seems to hold true for music consumption as well. An examination of the data from Brazil, where three families were interviewed, for example, revealed some very distinct forms of musical consumption. Although Giovanna's family appeared to be the least musically inclined of all participating Brazilian families, their consumption of music depicted not only a particular lifestyle, but was more associated with listening activities. Their preference for *sertanejo* (i.e., a Brazilian genre that can be compared to country music), was consistent with stereotypes of this genre, being more associated with a particular lifestyle involving rural areas, horseback riding, rodeos, and so on (Ilari, 2007). By contrast, the families of Maiara and Giovani took part in many collective, "traditional" Brazilian musical practices such as *capoeira* and *maracatu*, which, in turn, affected their patterns of musical consumption. That is, the latter included listening to specific repertoires from Brazilian popular music, attending specific performances and acquiring a wide range of musical instruments and recordings. Needless to say, these patterns of musical consumption helped to maintain the status quo, and were highly influenced by the social spheres in which families navigated.

Along the same lines, Pugh (2009) argued that the key to understanding consumer culture in childhood lies in the meanings implicit in children's (and parents') social experiences. Pugh coined the term "economy of dignity" to define a system of social meanings associated with children's consumer culture. According to her, children everywhere "claim, contest, and exchange amongst themselves the terms of their social belonging, or just what it would take to be able to participate among their peers" (Pugh, 2009, p. 6). A closer look at our data suggests that the ways children consumed music played a role in the construction of their economy of dignity, and thus, their social lives. The Spanish mother, for example, spoke of music as a prop for her daughter to make friends while in school: "The CD we've got in the car, she wants to learn it by heart so that she can sing it at school. Music is a prop for her, do you follow? A prop for making friends, for dancing." Likewise, the Danish mother spoke at length about her daughter Catherine's social use of music, which, once again, translates well into Pugh's economy of dignity:

> She's also using it [music] in a very social way with her friends actually. It's not that she sets the trend . . . but you can use [it] for a lot of things without having anything in your hands. You can bring it everywhere and it's a great tool to have. And it attracts a lot of people. And that can be used in many contexts. In our recreation garden she is exposed to music. We also have the computer out there and everything. But there are also a lot of people out there who play music. And when there is a party someone always has a guitar on the lap. There is this guy called Thomas, he's a musician, he works as a music teacher. And he always has an instrument. . . . Catherine do you remember what instrument he just gave us? What did he call it? A nose flute. I've never seen something like that before. Maybe you can show it later. It's actually quite hard. It was Catherine's half brother, who cracked the code. It was very good. So, that's a good thing too. But it's more the community.

Musical consumption, then, was not only a synonym of social class and choice but also a way for children to position themselves within the many communities of practice (Wenger, 2000) in which they navigated (see Takahashi, 2013). Far from being neutral, these acts of consumption also revealed both implicit and explicit family beliefs, values, and ideologies, which were being transmitted to children, in many cases, without full awareness that this was happening.

Middle-Class Musical Childhoods: Global and Local Issues

In my analysis of data, I aimed to understand how middle-class children and families in different parts of the world engage with music. This was no simple task.

From the start, it was clear that the data would reveal a wide range of experiences. Research team members were thus urged to be cautious not to overinterpret the findings based on their own cultural biases and experiences. Still it was clear to me that some similarities would emerge across families. Perhaps the most important similarity was the fact that all parents meant well and strove to provide quality musical opportunities for their children. For some this meant giving in to the social pressures that have been associated with "good parenting" in the West (Furedi, 2001) such as enrolling children in a wide range of age-appropriate musical activities and/or worrying about cultivating children's musical talents and abilities as they develop and grow (e.g., Taiwan, Singapore, United States), even if this represented a huge commitment in terms of time and money. For others, this simply meant to let children experience music as part of everyday life, as a family/community activity (e.g., Denmark, two families in Brazil, the UK). In other words, while all parents in the study seemed to value music, the level of parental interest and involvement in children's music learning experiences—formal and informal—varied considerably. Yet, expectations regarding music learning seemed to be much stronger in families where parents themselves were musicians—amateurs and professionals (e.g., Israel, Singapore, two families in Brazil, one family in the Netherlands)—than in other families (e.g., UK, Kenya, one family in Brazil). Furthermore, even if autonomy, self-direction, and choice in music were cherished, the degree to which they were exercised also varied considerably across participating families, especially where music listening and instrument selection/formal music learning were concerned. This is consistent with the idea that different cultures value different degrees of autonomy and compliance in children, as previously documented (Bidjerano and Newman, 2010).

Differences between time spent in organized activities and parental anxieties about their children's futures were also notorious. The musical life of the "über busy" Taiwanese Annie, who listened to classical music at home, learned the cello, and attended several live performances stood in stark contrast, for example, to the less structured musical life of Brazilian Giovanna, which revolved around listening to *sertanejo* songs with "adult content," usually in the company of her father, while taking horseback riding lessons or helping at the veterinarian clinic owned by her family. Thus, children's musical lives took on many shapes: some were afforded more opportunities to engage in formal music education than others. Still, music was omnipresent in children's lives, and parents seemed to value it, either for its own sake, like the British, Danish, and Kenyan parents, who talked at length about the enjoyment of music, or as a means to influence learning experiences in other areas (e.g., US and Taiwanese parents).

The other interesting aspect that emerged from the data referred to musical consumption in urban middle-class homes. Digital media and commercial music, available in the form of CDs, DVDs, toys, and digital recordings existed in all homes, although in different quantities. In some families, parents closely monitored children's use of them, especially when their acquisition involved live streaming on computers and other technological devices. Older siblings played an important role here, helping parents control inappropriate content and modeling good behaviors. Yet, in other families, parents appeared to be less worried about repertoire selection, or simply did not mention it in their interviews. But overall, it was clear that heavy corporate marketing strategies have made their way into middle-class households across the world. This is far from surprising, in that we live in times of globalization and rapid information exchange (see Buckingham, 2011; Fleer, Hedegaard, and Tudge, 2009). Children in the study were familiar with or owned Disney movies, DVDs of musicals, digital players, and other items of musical consumption, which, at times, were used as icons of their economy of dignity (Pugh, 2009).

But it seems to me that what was most interesting here was how childhood appeared to be constructed in different families, societies, and cultures. Conceptions of children and childhood held by parents varied considerably, in spite of the fact that parental discourses and practices revolved, to some extent, around locally articulated forms of autonomy, self-direction, choice, concerted cultivation, and musical consumption. Some perceived childhood as a time of intensive preparation to thrive in adulthood, following the idea that children live through a process of becoming. Others viewed childhood predominantly as a special and separate period in life, marked by a fair amount of play and enjoyment. Still others appeared to be caught right between them, at times indicating an ambiguous separation between the worlds of adults and children. These different conceptions were reflected in the musical parenting of the participating children.

Conclusions

Social class plays a role in the construction of musical childhoods worldwide. Urban, middle-class musical childhoods appear to be marked by a certain degree of parental involvement, which is directly linked to parental perceptions of music (including preferences), beliefs concerning children's autonomy and self-direction, beliefs regarding formal music learning, and acts of consumption. These, in turn, are both personal and social constructions that depend on local and global values, cultural beliefs and practices, and affordances. Thus, social class is more than an independent variable. It is necessary for music education research to make an effort to understand how social class influences music learning in homes, schools, and communities, because there are many implications of this research for practice. Are working-class musical childhoods similar to middle-class musical childhoods? Does cultural orientation (Triandis, 1995) influence the way in which middle-class childhoods are constructed? In other words, do middle-class children in collectivist cultures experience music differently than their peers in individualistic cultures? These questions require urgent investigation because they have a direct influence on what happens—musically and extramusically—in homes, communities, and classrooms.

SECTION III
New Ideas

7 Nurturing the Musical "Open-Earedness" of Seven-Year-Olds

Diane Persellin

TODAY'S SEVEN-YEAR-OLD CHILDREN exhibit openness and excitement about many genres of musical styles experienced in their everyday lives and in their ever widening world. As these young children from around the world are growing out of their early childhood, they continue to enjoy singing, dancing, moving, and playing at home or on the playground alone or with extended family members as they have since they were toddlers. Many still delight in sharing songs that they have learned at school from their friends and teachers, at home from their parents and siblings, or as they begin to participate in music lessons. Some seven-year-olds still enjoy creating their own spontaneous songs much as they did when they were younger. Music is an important part of their expanding world.

In this digital age, many seven-year olds also now relish singing and dancing to their iPods, television programs, boom boxes, electronic games, computers, and other modern musical toys and instruments. They collect CDs, DVDs, and MP3s of their favorite music. Increasingly, these children learn from popular culture through radio and television programs, from observing older siblings and parents engaged in music technology, and from imitating and emulating popular tunes and advertisement jingles (Campbell and Lum, 2007). Johnson-Green and Custodero (2002) noted the powerful response that music in the media elicits from children as young as one and two. In a large study with over two thousand eight- to eighteen-year-olds in the United States, eight-year-old children were found to listen to a variety of types of music an average of one hour per day (Roberts, Foehr, and Rideout, 2005).

Young children and their parents enthusiastically support diverse genres of digital music. One label, Baby Rock caters to parents in their thirties and forties and features renditions of lullabies and early childhood songs in the style of the Cure, the Beach Boys, and Metallica (La Gorce, 2006). Another popular recording company, Putumayo Kids, was created to introduce children to cultures of the world through music and has become one of the world's leading children's record labels. Amazon.com and iTunes feature hundreds of classical music recordings of many categories and traditions targeting young listeners.

This enthusiasm, acceptance, and preference for a wide variety of musical genres by young children have been topics of great interest. Hargreaves (1982) has labeled this characteristic as "open-earedness" and found that children under the age of five are accepting of many genres of music. He has found that this open-earedness appears to wane as children grow older and become less tolerant of a broader range of music in favor of popular music. As they develop, nine- and ten-year-old children may become more interested in popular music that is shared by their peers and family members and reinforced by media.

Several children who were interviewed for our project exhibited broad and eclectic musical interests as seven-year-olds. Would they maintain these interests in diverse music styles and genres over the next few years of their lives? Would active participation in age-appropriate music classes, lessons, and experiences support their broad interests or would their interest narrow as they aged? In this chapter, I review the literature examining the evidence of open-earedness of young children and the studies documenting how this interest wanes as children age. I discuss music preferences and open-earedness of two seven-year-olds in the United States. As an extension of this study, three years later I revisited the two US children who had participated in the MyPlace, MyMusic project again as ten-year olds to interview them and their parents to determine whether their music preferences and open-earedness had changed over the course of three years and, if so, what the influences were that contributed to these changes.

The Open-Earedness Theory

In the early 1980s, Hargreaves (1982) examined aesthetic reactions to music with groups of children from seven to fifteen years old as well as in a study with children four to seven years old (Hargreaves, 1987). He found age-related changes in liking for unfamiliar melodies with a significant decrease from ages four to five to ages six to seven. Based on his research, he coined the term "open-earedness" to describe younger children's tendency to be more "open-eared" to forms of music regarded by older listeners as "unconventional." He found an aesthetic openness to more types of music in younger children before these wider and more accepting habits began to wane by age six and the music window appeared to narrow.

Hargreaves and LeBlanc led studies to extend this initial research with additional studies on open-earedness (Hargreaves, North, and Tarrant, 2006; LeBlanc, 1991; LeBlanc, Sims, Siivola, and Obert, 1996) suggesting that (a) younger children are more open-eared and are less likely to reject classical music or music of an unfamiliar style, and (b) open-earedness declines as the child enters adolescence. Five-year-old children had a high level of preference and liked many types of music, but preference levels then declined to a low point at age ten.

Gembris and Schellberg (2003) also found evidence for an open-earedness effect. The authors investigated preferences of elementary school children for music of four different styles (classical, ethnic, avant-garde, and pop). For the preference measurement, they used a sound questionnaire and an iconographic rating scale (smiley-face scale). The authors found an increase in disliking for classical music for children seven to ten years old and a constant level of liking for popular music. The ratings for avant-garde and ethnic music remained constant from first to third grades (in the scale of "liking") and moved to disliking by the age of ten. Schellberg and Gembris (2004) confirmed these results in a second study. With increasing age, all pieces of music were judged more negatively. These changes in preferences were highly significant regarding all types of music. Kopiez and Lehmann (2008) also found a decline of open-earedness for unconventional music (i.e., classical, ethnic, and avant-garde music) between the ages of seven and eight years.

Brunger (1984) also found an open-earedness for unfamiliar styles of music with younger children, declining gradually with increasing age. He found that this open-earedness disappeared in most children by the age of nine. One example of this trend involved a Mozart aria. More than half of the five- and six-year-olds liked the Mozart aria, but with each additional year, the dislike of this music grew more strongly. Similar patterns emerged for examples of the classical music of Bach, Mozart, and Mendelssohn as well as twentieth-century art music and ethnic music. Younger pupils indicated liking for this music. By the age of ten, however, children indicated a strong rejection of these types of music. The results confirm an open-earedness for unfamiliar styles of music among the younger children, but this declines with increasing age. Other investigators have confirmed that younger children routinely gave higher preference scores for all recorded musical excerpts that they listened to, and responded more positively to all musical excerpts presented than did older children (Brittin, 2000; LeBlanc et al., 1996; Montgomery, 1996; Sloboda, 2001).

Does this open-earedness in children wane in favor of popular music? In a longitudinal study (Schellberg, 2006), 109, seven- and eight-year-olds rated their likes or dislikes of ten short pieces of music that were representative of a range of different music styles (vocal music—operetta and opera excerpts, instrumental classical music, pop music, twentieth-century art music, and ethnic music). The same questionnaire was repeated one and two years later. Most of the seven-year-olds liked or tolerated the music, whereas the eight- and nine-year-old children reacted more negatively to all excerpts except pop music.

Children's increasing preference for popular and rock styles of music has been found to increase with age (Brittin, 2000; Greer, Dorow, and Randall, 1974;

Jellison and Flowers, 1991; LeBlanc, 1979, 1981; Roberts, Foehr, and Rideout, 2005). Children also prefer music—popular, rock, and other styles performed in faster tempi (LeBlanc, 1981; LeBlanc et al., 1996; Montgomery, 1996). Minkenberg (1991) noted that music examples with fast tempi and "suitability for dancing" were highly rated. Sims and Cassidy's study (1997) also demonstrated that the absence or presence of lyrics did not appear to affect young children's music preferences.

In a broader qualitative study, Roulston (2006) examined music preferences of children three to eight years old through conversations and interviews with parents and children and observations of classroom settings in day-care and elementary classrooms. She found that (1) children expressed distinct preferences for an eclectic range of music from a very early age; (2) popular and rock music were frequently mentioned as preferred styles by parents and children, with movie and television soundtracks also ranking high in popularity; and (3) music listening and experiences in the home described by children and parents differed considerably from what was offered in school and day-care settings. Sims and Cassidy (1997) came to an even broader conclusion that young children's music attitudes and preferences do not seem to be based on specific musical characteristics and that children may have very idiosyncratic responses and listening styles.

If children's tendencies toward open-earedness is closing and shifting in favor of popular and rock music, can their music preferences be modified? Several investigators have studied the possibility of modifying music preferences of children using several different treatments. These treatments have included passive repeated exposure to unfamiliar music as well as through age-appropriate active music instruction. Schuckert and McDonald (1968) asked children four to six years old to indicate an initial preference for one of two distinct types of music (classical or jazz). For the next four days, children passively listened to their least preferred music for five minutes while doing an unrelated task. Children were then retested to determine shifts in musical preference. Although half of the children slightly increased their liking of their least preferred music, the results were not significant. This study, however, did not invite the children to move, interact, or participate in instruction with the music.

Conversely, Carper (2001) did incorporate active music instruction in his study. He presented four types of music, American popular music, children's music, Western classical music, and traditional Japanese music to young children, ages three to seven. Half of the children passively listened to the music. The other half of the children actively participated in six early childhood instructional sessions, each lasting thirty minutes. Children who actively participated in the instruction were significantly more likely to have increased preferences for the unfamiliar music. With the exception of popular music, which started at the highest level of preference and then slipped a few points following treatment, the other three types of music all increased on the preference scale with the Japanese music increasing the most. While the unfamiliar style of the Japanese music was initially less preferred than the other three types of music, it increased to the level of Western classical music. Older children in the study, the seven-year olds, indicated the strongest preference for popular music. The younger children, three- to six-year-olds, were still more open to all four types of music.

In two additional studies (McKoy, 2003; Shehan, 1984), music instruction did not increase preference for world music to a level corresponding with initial preferences for popular music with eight- to ten-year-olds. However, students' preferences for world music after instruction did increase and were comparable to preinstruction preferences for Western classical music. Fung and Gromko (2001) found the most dramatic change. In their study, children ages seven to twelve, who were actively moving and drawing to unfamiliar Korean music, greatly increased their preference for the music (94 percent) compared to children who passively listened to the same music (52 percent).

In summary, young children are receptive to a wide range of styles of music. This open-earedness has been found to begin declining at about age five and continues declining until about the age of nine or ten. As children's preferences begin to narrow, interest in popular and rock music increases, undoubtedly influenced by children's easy access to music through the media. While repeated exposure to unfamiliar music through passive listening has not been found successful in modifying children's music preferences, some investigators have been successful in modifying musical preferences of children through active music instruction. This study gives a closer snapshot of four young children at the age of seven and again at ten to determine whether the open-earedness theory applies to them and to gain some insight into the musical lives of these young children.

The Original Data: Open-Earedness and the Seven-Year-Olds

All seven-year-old children around the world who participated in the MyPlace, MyMusic project reported diverse interests in music (see Andang'o and Pacheco, chapter 4, this volume; Young, chapter 1, this volume). While the investigators may have selected children they knew were interested in music, the wide range of interests was striking. Many of the seventeen children cited traditional children's songs, popular children's songs, and kiddie rock songs as favorites. Their parents confirmed these interests and gave examples of these more traditional musical interests. In addition, however, children and their parents shared examples of interest in music such as classical, opera, solo cello, country western, worship, ethnic dance, school music, popular radio music, Byzantine chants from a nearby monastery, musical theater, songs from television, Broadway, and folk ballads.

Some of the interviewed parents were aware of this "open-earedness" of their child and were delighted by it. The mother of Sissi in Israel stated:

> I can put on CDs of all kinds of music and Sissi won't say to me, "Hey, what is that stuff?" She won't say that. It's like with Bobby McFerrin: she simply sat with me and studied his website. We really researched him. We saw more and more details. And she also listened to Bach. It does something good for her. She has no prejudices about things. . . . I can play the CD of "Carmen" and start to sing and tell her the story. *The Magic Flute* was the same way. I told her the story. She watched it and has seen it three times already without me. . . . She doesn't need much mediation [introduction]. A one-time mediation is enough for her and then it will open her imagination and she's already there [engaged].

Sissi, as a seven-year-old, also stated that she was a fan of film music, Bobby McFerrin, Bach, Grieg, and other classical music. She would delight in singing songs after just listening to an adult choir rehearsal. She also enjoyed playing the piano and recorder.

Melina in Greece, also enjoyed a variety of music including Greek pop and dance music, theatrical performances with music, and ethnic dance music such as samba, mambo, salsa, and tango. She enjoyed listening to children's music on her CDs and playing the glockenspiel, piano, and toy guitar. When she studied and before she went to bed, she listened to classical music. She also reported that she enjoyed listening to Byzantine chant sung by monks at a nearby monastery. Her musical tastes as a seven-year-old appeared to be broad and eclectic.

The seven-year-olds in the United States who participated in this study also delighted in listening to and singing a variety of types of music. These children live in a beautiful suburban neighborhood near their private Montessori school in large city in the southwestern part of the country. They attend excellent music classes three times each week. Their second-grade classroom teacher also enjoys sharing his favorite music with the class. The mothers of each child work primarily in the home.

At age seven, Rose is a bright girl who loves all types of music: simple school songs taught in music class, complex songs from Broadway musicals taught by her classroom teacher, songs heard on television such as those from Hannah Montana played by Miley Cyrus, and songs her parents played on the their CD player in the kitchen. One of her favorite ways to enjoy music is to participate in the electronic *High School Musical* dancing game and was delighted to demonstrate that game for our interview. She especially likes to sing songs from these multiple sources on her swing set in the backyard.

While Rose's mother stated she does not feel that she nor her husband are particularly musical, they are interested in having Rose introduced to music and hope that she will play the piano. They introduced her to the Baby Einstein CD series of classical music at an early age because they felt it was important for her to become familiar with classical music. Her father enjoys singing country western songs with her, especially those sung by Randy Travis, a popular country

Figure 7.1. Score for "Snail, Snail" (traditional American song).

western singer. Rose's classroom teacher enjoys teaching his class Broadway and standard popular classic songs such as, "Somewhere over the Rainbow" from the musical film *The Wizard of Oz* and "Swinging on a Star" from the film *Going My Way.*

When asked to demonstrate her school songs, Rose sang the two-note song "Snail, Snail" accurately and musically (Figure 7.1). But when she ventured out to the backyard to demonstrate her favorite place to make music on the swing set, she became fully engaged in the more challenging and diverse Broadway music, singing with great enthusiasm and expression. She appeared to have forgotten about the interview and was only aware of her singing of these favorite songs. The swinging motion appeared to inspire her singing.

Brad attends the same private school as Rose and has the same teachers. Although his parents do not claim to be musical, they enrolled him in an early childhood music program and then in violin and piano starting at age five. Brad has a large toy box dedicated to music toys and an impressive collection of electronic games. He proudly shows off his collection of seventy-two CDs that he plays in his purple boom box. In addition, he has an iPod nano full of popular and children's music as well as music games. His mother reports that he loves to sing in the car and in his bedroom. His favorite toy appears to be the Cha Cha Slide, an electronic game with a rock music accompaniment and verbal dance instructions. He was happy to sing, "Here Comes a Bluebird" with perfect intonation for the interview and then improvised a simple melody using sol–fa syllables and hand signs. When he set up the electronic floor music game, Cha Cha Slide, however, he became more excited and would have continued to dance all evening following the verbal instructions and rock music on this electronic game. He jumped, hopped, clapped, and twirled and was thoroughly engaged by the challenge.

Returning Three Years Later: Interests

Three years later, I followed up and interviewed these two children and their mothers in the United States again to determine whether the children's musical interests had changed. Because these children were local, I was also able to interview the music teacher who had taught them twice each week over the course of the past three years. I asked the children and their mothers the same questions from the original MyPlace, MyMusic project. I also then reminded the children, their mothers, and their music teacher of the children's responses when they were seven-years-old and asked if and how these interests had changed and evolved. Because I was so interested in the changes and development of musical interests and preferences of these two children in the United States, I decided to interview two other children from the original project. I selected two children who, as seven-year-olds, exhibited a wide range of music preferences: Melina in Greece and Sissi in Israel. To do so, I contacted the local investigators who assisted me in providing introductions to the young girls and their mothers. I was able to ask them my questions via e-mail. In each of these cases, the local investigators knew the children personally so were able to offer additional insights about the music activities of these girls. My questions were the same as those asked in the initial MyPlace, MyMusic project and also how their musical tastes and preferences had changed over the past three years. The children and their mothers were delighted to share the current musical interests of these girls and how they had changed since they were seven.

Melina in Greece, who loved Byzantine chants and classical music, is now ten years old and is more interested in Greek pop music than her more eclectic tastes as a seven-year-old. She no longer discusses an interest in Byzantine chant or other more diverse types of music, and is now much more focused on the popular music that she shares with her friends and siblings. She does not participate in formal music classes or activities outside of school, so she has limited opportunities to reinforce her earlier interest in classical music and early Byzantine chant.

Sissi in Israel who loved opera and other classical music three years ago as a seven-year-old is now an enthusiastic fan of pop music. Her favorite artist is the British pop singer, Adele. Her mother hears her singing, dancing, and jumping on the bed to this music in her bedroom. She enjoys sharing this music with her older teenage sister. She has continued to take guitar lessons. Sissi claims to have lost all interest in opera and classical music, but her mother disagrees. At a recent guitar lesson, Sissi's teacher played a recording of an Albeniz guitar concerto. Sissi was fascinated by the piece and listened to it over and over again. She continues to listen to classical music in the privacy of her own room. Her mother feels that she still loves classical music even if she is unwilling to admit this at the age of ten.

In the United States, Brad's mother and music teacher agreed that Brad's broad musical repertoire and interests have narrowed somewhat now that he is ten years old, and these are now much more focused on rock and pop music. He confirmed that he is very enthusiastic about the electronic dance music of deadmau5 (pronounced "dead mouse") and in several interviews he could not think of any other music that he currently enjoys. However, Brad continues to enthusiastically participate in after-school music ensembles such as an instrumental tone chime choir and a community vocal choir. These programs are nurturing his broader musical interests even though he is reluctant to admit that he is delighted with these extracurricular music programs. While Brad is eager to describe his interest in the popular music of deadmau5, he continues to participate enthusiastically in extracurricular music activities that focus primarily on classical and folk music. These ensembles are keeping his musical interests broad and more open.

Rose's musical interests continue to expand as an active ten-year-old girl. Currently, she is involved in her school choir, a tone chime after-school ensemble, and in a community children's chorus that performs with the local professional symphony orchestra. She takes great pride in these performance opportunities and delights in what she is learning in these extracurricular programs as well in her music class at school. At home, she eagerly listens to her favorite performer, the popular country western musician Taylor Swift. This interest continues to reflect her father's loyalty to the country western genre. Rose is also a fan of the teenage favorite rock band, Neon Trees. Her mother reported that Rose is "an avid watcher of *American Idol* and other musical television shows like that." Her mother reports that she still sings all of the time and her vocal repertoire heard in the house is wide and varied. Her music teacher says that Rose continues to be interested in all music. Clearly, Rose continues to be "open-eared."

Summary

All four of these children had strong and diverse musical preferences as seven-year-olds. They were all beginning to enjoy some popular and rock music, and they also appeared to be delighted with other types of music including school folk songs, Broadway musicals, Byzantine chant, opera, country western music, and ethnic dance music. When revisited three years later, they all cited an even stronger interest in popular and rock music. Rose, Sissi, and Brad also demonstrated an interest in genres of music other than the popular music enjoyed by their peers, although they were reluctant to admit this. On more careful examination, their broader musical interests exhibited at seven years old have not disappeared and are arguably increasing. Perhaps their active participation in private music lessons, after-school choirs, instrumental ensembles, music making in the home, and quality music instruction in school has kept alive this interest in and openness to diverse music. As a ten-year-old, only Melina appears to be less interested in a wider range of music. She is not participating in formal music lessons or classes outside of school and appears to be focused only on the popular music of her peers and siblings. Because a systematic and controlled assessment of unfamiliar music was not conducted with these and other children at the age of seven and again at the age of ten, it is impossible to be more conclusive about these findings.

Conclusions

Music plays an important role in human development, enhancing the growth of cognition and emotional response. It enhances children's play and may be an important means for them to learn about their world (Campbell and Lum, 2007). Rich experiences with a wide variety of music at an early age may provide a higher quality of human experience throughout a person's lifetime (Flohr and Persellin, 2011).

We have evidence that young children's ears and minds are open to a wide variety of genres of music before this interest begins to narrow in favor of music preferred by their peers or embraced by their families. It may be possible, however, that children's open-earedness can be nurtured and their musical preferences can be modified. While Schuckert and McDonald (1968) found that musical preferences cannot be changed by passive listening to music, other investigators (Carper, 2001; Fung and Gromko, 2001) found that age-appropriate music instruction that includes singing, moving, and actively listening to a wide variety of music has the potential to change and expand music preferences in children. When children are interacting with the music in relevant ways, they may become more tolerant and accepting of that music. In addition, an enthusiastic parent or older sibling may nurture a deepening interest in a specific genre of music in the home.

Children learn more quickly in the first few years of life than at any other time. The early years of childhood represent a significant period for enhancing verbal, cognitive, physical, and musical development. This period of rapid development establishes a base for future learning. Some past interests and experiences are maintained when nurtured while novel interests are introduced and embraced (Hviid 2012). Applied to music, the acquisition of a rich and diverse repertoire of music when children are the most open can be an important part of childhood. Parents and educators can then encourage and build on the natural positive relationship that young children have with this rich storehouse of music by providing active age-appropriate music experiences for children as they develop.

Never before have we had such plentiful access to such a wide diversity of music. In the home, parents can easily download nearly any type of music from the internet. Television offers hundreds of channels with many music programs. Today children enjoy more access to concerts and live music in their communities. While some parents are taking advantage of this broad array of music, others rely on more familiar genres such as baby rock and the music that harkens back to the sounds of their own teen years. Parents are encouraged to share excellent and diverse types of music, recorded and live, with their children of all ages. Children delight in making music with their parents, so mothers and fathers should not be shy about singing and dancing with them.

At school, teachers can also make a concerted effort to share a wide variety of excellent music that includes opera, world music, jazz, avant-garde, and a variety of classical music. This unfamiliar and intriguing music can be introduced and reinforced through age-appropriate hands-on instruction that includes singing, moving, actively listening, and composing simple responses to this music on classroom instruments.

While we have a rich literature about young children's musical preferences, there is still much to be learned. Pop and media music are becoming more universal via the internet, television, and movies, but the music preferences of young children may still differ by effects of age, country, and gender. Further study of the development, narrowing, and nurturing of children's music preferences would make a valuable contribution to the field. This work could help parents and teachers decide how and when to introduce children to unfamiliar music and how to keep children open and enthusiastic about a broad variety of musical genres.

8 Musical Childhoods in South Africa

"The Times They Are a-Changin"

Sheila C. Woodward

A RAINBOW NATION at the southern tip of Africa, ablaze with a diversity of colors and cultures, sees many children today enjoying lives once barely imaginable. Until two decades ago, South African society had long been forcibly split along racial lines that denied the majority of children many basic human rights. I was born into a political era dominated by a policy euphemistically known as "Separate Development," or "Apartheid," in which children lived in neighborhoods restricted to their own race (Giliomee and Mbenga, 2007; Thompson, 2001). I attended school with children of the same skin color. If I went to the city, I would travel in a section of a bus or train according to my racial designation. Waiting with my parents to buy a stamp at the post office, I might have a chance to see a child of another race at a distance, as lines were segregated. On a daily basis, I usually saw only white children like me at church, on the beach, in a restaurant, or at the cinema.

At the age of seventeen, I attended a summer camp run by a British-based organization that broke the mold by including teenagers of different races. I made my first friends across the color bar. An extraordinary explosion of excitement, fear, and daring characterized the days that followed. We caused our parents untold anguish as we boldly (yet nervously) visited each other's homes, churches, and social events. We were a young generation ready to take on a regime that had dictated our segregated childhoods to that point. Parents argued against our wanting to sit at the same dinner table. They warned against any romantic liaisons. They worried what the neighbors would think. They were terrified we would be arrested.

Suddenly, in the midst of that final high school year of 1976, South African children across the nation marched out of their schools into the city streets, chanting and *toyi-toying* in protest against recent laws enforcing language restrictions in education.[1] They would likely have been most concerned with an immediate struggle to pass exams in a language not their own. But some of us were thinking about the long-term effect of disadvantages to black children in gaining entrance to universities and professions in which they could someday challenge the government. This generation of children catapulted an underground freedom struggle into a tumultuous torrent of open action. While some teenagers were rioting, facing torture in prison, or fighting on the borders, others of us were bucking the social systems. We went as racially mixed groups to concerts at the city hall, sang together in churches, and attended social dances at schools, always taunting the social status quo. We went to Des and Dawn Lindburgh's daring private production of *Godspell*, with musicians of all races on the stage. Many children were joining mixed audiences for the first time or discovering the music of the multiracial pop band, Juluka. Music was playing the role of "mirror, mediator and prophet" (Byerly, 1998, p. 1). In the 1980s, the music of multiracial Mango Groove topped the hit parades and members of the Cape Town Philharmonic Orchestra teamed up with local Amampondo musicians to form Intsholo, creating new sounds with brass, *djembes*, and African marimbas. Life in South Africa would never be the same, musically, or otherwise.

Now, eighteen years after the first fully inclusive elections ushered Nelson Mandela into the presidency, I joined the MyPlace, MyMusic research team and conducted an investigation into the musical lives of two seven-year-old, middle-class children in South Africa. I began by contemplating how different any such study might have been during my childhood years. As a middle-class white seven-year-old, I had proudly worn the uniform of a public girls' school of six hundred students that boasted several music teachers at any given time. My musical life at that age centered on weekly school individual lessons in piano, plus group lessons in singing, Orff Schulwerk, Dalcroze Eurythmics, and ballet. We sang a hymn at the start of each school day. At church services, hymns were accompanied by a magnificent organ, followed by Sunday school where a teacher accompanied songs at the piano. We sang campfire songs at Girl Guides (a branch of the Scouting movement), and attended Scottish Country Dance lessons. I remember gathering around the gramophone record player in our lounge, singing along to music from films that enthralled us, such as *The Sound of Music* and *Snow White and the Seven Dwarfs*. We listened to children's programs on the radio, with songs like "The Teddy Bear's Picnic" that are still firmly etched into my memory. Traveling in the Valiant automobile on long family vacations through breathtaking scenery, my father kept us entertained with songs about "three little fishies" who "swam right out to sea." When my grandparents visited for Sunday lunch, I would give them a recital of my latest piano pieces. At the age of seven, I never considered what black children might be doing, or what songs they might be singing. I had never been able to spend time with any of these children. I later learned that, while music existed officially in school curricula for white, black, colored, and Indian children (each racial group was assigned to one of four separate departments of education), not all children enjoyed substantial formal music education in their schools. I learned that although the abundance of music education available at my school was not something children of other races typically experienced, they had nevertheless tended to enjoy rich musical environments within their own cultural communities, often developing their musical skills outside of formal schooling (Blacking, 1973, 1995; Gibson, Norris, and Alcock, 1992).

Theoretical Framework and Method

In contemplating possible characteristics of a child's musical life in South Africa today, I began considering the wide diversity of cultures within the country. No one child could possibly be seen as typical. Even if one were to randomly select hundreds of children across the country, there would be multiple cultures represented and further subcultures within those (Giliomee and Mbenga, 2007; Magubane, 1998). I considered how the musical lives of any study participants would conceivably reflect the cultures of their families. Their musical worlds would surely be influenced by their parents' cultural values and norms. It seemed appropriate, therefore, to base this study on the cultural-ecological theories described by Jonathan Tudge (2008) in his multinational study of middle-class toddlers, *The Everyday Lives of Young Children*. He explains that, in exploring the lives of children, it is

> relatively easy to see the ways in which parents and other people attempt to ensure that they become skilled in the practices that are considered important and to learn the values, concepts and ways of behaving that are valued in the culture in which the children are situated. It is possible to see this by examining the types of activities in which children are encouraged to participate. . . . It can also be seen from examining the types of settings into which young children are placed, the lessons they are asked to learn, the behaviors they are asked to practice, and the skills they are expected to master. All of these things are intrinsically linked to the culture in which children are being raised. (Tudge, 2008, p. 1)

Tudge suggests that examining children's everyday activities allows us to see the links between culture and human development (p. 274). He also urges us to not lose sight of what the individual brings to the experiences at hand. Many theories show the connections between children's immediate cultural groups and their individual development (Vygotsky, 1935/1994; Weisner, 1996). Nevertheless, children's development is not only the product of culture. Children do not simply receive cultural messages; they interpret based on their own individual differences (Goodnow and Collins, 1990). Therefore, I assumed that participants would naturally present a musical world characterized by the immediate cultural milieu that is, nevertheless, unique, due to the individuality of the child concerned. No visit to any other child, even in a very similar cultural environment, would offer exactly the same findings. With this ontological assumption in mind, this exploration aimed to highlight how the musical worlds of two South African children were linked to their parents' cultures and to what their parents encourage, reflecting their values and beliefs. I was particularly interested in the ways through which children's musical activities are shaped by parental choices for the child, based on what they deem important and valuable.

The reader might question the emphasis on middle-class children; however, it ties in with the focus of the MyPlace, MyMusic original protocol, as outlined in the introduction to this volume. Furthermore, the need for such studies is exhorted by Tudge who points out how researchers have frequently concentrated their studies of black or African children on low-income populations and that "attention needs to be given to the early experiences of Black children from middle-class or wealthy families" (Tudge, 2008, p .19). In no way does this investigation imply any sort of generalization of the results nor does it seek to classify societies. However, value may be contributed from its discoveries when placed alongside multiple other studies, as it adds a miniature piece to a mural that informs our overall knowledge base.

Locating Participants

I decided to go back to the tree-lined, mountain-view neighborhood where I lived as a child, to explore the musical life of a child attending one of its local schools today. It was also the same suburb of a major city where I had returned to live as a young mother with two small children. My own children were able to enjoy the benefits of my generation's struggle, sitting at school desks and singing in choirs with children of diverse cultures. Now my children are grown and a new generation of children lives in those same houses and attends those schools. In order to find child participants, I contacted music teachers at several schools in the area, briefly explaining the study and asking for an introduction to a seven-year-old student. A teacher at a school for boys (the "brother" school of the girls' school I had attended) was quick to respond with several names and I began contacting the parents to see if they would allow me to conduct the interview. Two parents responded immediately with such touching enthusiasm that I decided to interview both these children.

Interview Design

In adapting the general, MyPlace, MyMusic interview protocol, I considered the opening questions posed by Tudge (2008), which asked precisely what I wanted to know about these children, with specific reference to their musical lives: "How do young children spend their time? Who are the people with whom children are engaged in activities and interaction? In which sorts of activities do they get involved, and how do these activities get started? Where do they spend their time?" (Tudge 2008, p. 1). To maintain an informal atmosphere that would likely be less intimidating to a child, I did not read from a script. I kept the overarching questions in mind as I asked questions from memory and improvised others that arose within the conversation. The planned questions were designed to elicit information along the lines of data already collected in existing MyPlace, MyMusic studies (e.g., Ilari, 2013a; Young, 2012b): sources of musical stimulation in the home; parental musical background, musical instruments, media available in the home, favorite repertoires, engagement in organized activities and descriptions of family musical activities (Ilari, chapter 6, this volume; Koutsoupidou, chapter 5, this volume).

Jason, the First Participant

Jason is a seven-year-old attending first grade in a boys' public school funded with supplemental fees paid by parents, in an upmarket suburb of Cape Town. It is a long-established school, with extensive buildings, landscaping, and sports fields. As in the days when I attended school in this neighborhood, it is widely considered to offer one of the best educations possible in the country. In all my days of walking down that street, I only ever saw white boys passing through those school gates. However, the changes in the country's constitution that took place after the 1994 elections led to an increasingly diverse student population enrolled in its most prestigious schools.

Jason is the son of two professionals, a mother who works in information technology and a father in insurance. When they were children, these parents lived in a considerably less affluent neighborhood. After their marriage, they purchased a home in an area previously restricted to whites, now free of racial restrictions. They later purchased their current spacious home, surrounded by well-manicured lawns, trees, and flowering plants. The brick house has several bedrooms, several living areas, and a double garage for the cars. They have robust security systems—high walls, electric gates, and a private company monitoring neighborhood security. Jason has one brother nine years old living in the home with him and his parents.

Sources of Musical Stimulation in the Home

Jason and his brother are encouraged to practice for thirty minutes daily on their digital keyboard. They complete weekly music theory homework, asking their mother for help when needed. She describes how, during the holidays, they tend to "make up their own stuff" on the keyboard.

The family makes music together before the children go to bed, singing church songs with their father accompanying them on guitar. Jason and his mother speak with obvious joy about this experience. Family relatives visit on holidays, bringing instruments with them. One of their favorite, most common holiday activities is making music together with their extended family.

Jason listens to music DVDs his parents have purchased, sometimes putting them into the DVD player himself, and other times his father doing this for him. I ask him which is his favorite and he says it is called *Supernatural.*[2] He sets up the equipment to allow me to experience it. The female Australian musician introducing the live concert announces this proudly as "Extreme Worship." The DVD shows a band playing Christian worship music at a live concert, with a large audience of youth dancing energetically to the music, arms waving in the air. Jason sits on the coffee table in front of the TV, eyes glued to the screen the entire time, his feet doing little bounces now and again. The piece plays almost to the end when Jason's head suddenly darts around to see if I am watching it. He had been engrossed in the music to that moment. His mother comments that Jason is normally on his feet, dancing and singing along to the DVD.

Jason takes me to another room in the house where he has an electronic device called Air Drums, which he received as a gift when he was five years old. He loves to play this. It takes Jason about ten minutes to set up the gadget, attaching all the wires, hooking two devices to his shoes and a control panel to his belt. He then picks up the mallets that are also attached with wires to the control panel, and begins drumming in the air as though he has imaginary drums in front of him. He also makes tapping movements with his feet. Various rhythmic percussion sounds can be heard whenever he moves his mallets and feet, although they appear to have a preprogrammed regular rhythm, not exactly matched to his movements. He makes changes on the control panel periodically to elicit different percussive sounds. Jason's smiles and animation betray the enormous pleasure he enjoys in this activity. This is clearly related to what he said earlier about wanting to learn the drums. His mother explains that "when he got the air drums as a present, every day he" [she demonstrates movements of playing drums].

We go to yet another room and Jason dances with a small hand-held musical toy given to him by a local, child-friendly restaurant. He calls it a rock and, when he dances with it in his hand, it plays a synthesized music recording. He also mentions a toy for singing, but does not know where to find it.

In this activity room, Jason switches on a TV and picks up the Wii devices—one in each hand—that he explains are controls for selecting songs, people, and instruments. He changes the timbres of the preprogrammed melodies, harmonies, and rhythms. Jason explains how he put himself into the program (we see a picture of him playing a guitar among the various people on the screen).

Parental Musical Background

Jason's father is a guitarist who regularly sings and plays his instrument in the home. His side of the family is very active musically and they read music. The uncle plays trumpet, saxophone, guitar, drums, and keyboard. Two aunts play guitar and one of them also plays keyboard. Jason's mother obviously enjoys music and participates in the family singing of church songs. She says she has had to teach herself music theory in order to assist her children with their theory homework study, but says her father is very musical, playing the keyboard by ear.

Musical Instruments

Jason has access to a Yamaha keyboard provided by his parents. It is on a stand and has a matching stool. Jason has obviously been taught to value the instrument highly as he very carefully removes the cover and replaces it again after practicing. Although Jason's father has a guitar that he plays daily while singing with the family, Jason makes no mention of having played it. Other instruments, such as saxophone and trumpet, are brought to the house and played by family members when they visit on vacation, and Jason enjoys hearing this live music.

Media Available in the Home

Jason engages in music through a variety of media in the home, including an iPad, iPhone, computer, TVs, Wii music games, musical toys, and DVD/CD player. The family listens to music on the radio when traveling in their car.

Favorite Repertoires

I learn that the music performed and listened to in the home is predominantly the music of the Pentecostal church to which the family belongs. Every evening, before bed and prayers, they sing worship songs together, the father accompanying the songs on the guitar. When I ask Jason if he will sing a favorite song for me, he ponders for a minute and then his mother reminds him about the songs they sing at night. He acknowledges this but still ponders for a while longer. She then reminds him of one that she knows he likes. She sings the first two lines (see first line in Figure 8.1) and then he gains the confidence to sing "We Bless Your Name." Jason sings the triple meter song with a strong, beautiful tone quality and quite good intonation. He gives a sudden huge smile when he is finished and looks proudly at his mother.

Then Jason remembers the songs he has learned at school for their stage musical production of *Aladdin* and he tells me about the song that has actions "Boo-

Figure 8.1. Score of opening phrase for "We Bless Your Name" (composer unknown).

gie Bugs."[3] I ask him to sing it for me and he climbs off his chair to stand in front of me. Jason sings this song through with no hesitation and seems to be having enormous fun doing dance movements and actions that match the words.

Jason has favorite pieces that he plays from Bastien's *Primer Piano Method* book. He takes his music books out of a music bag and he tells me the other bag belongs to his brother. His favorite piece is a well-known melody included in the book, "Jingle Bells," which is notated for the right hand only. He plays the piece for me proudly. Then he finds another piece that appears earlier in the book, which he says makes him think of dogs barking. I notice that Jason takes good care of his music books—he carefully puts them away in the bag before covering the piano and moving to the next room.

Engagement in Organized Activities

Jason's mother tells me about how he grew up since his earliest days in the musical activities of the church. Jason describes people playing guitar, drums, and keyboard at the church and singing. He especially likes it when they play the drums and it makes him feel that he also wants to play the drums.

When Jason and his family attended his older brother's first school orientation, they heard a performance of the school orchestra. His brother was enthralled and told his parents that he would like to play the violin. They applied two years running for him to take violin lessons at the school, but they were turned down both times. At the start of the third year, his mother went to speak with the class music teacher to see what could be done to achieve acceptance. She was very encouraging and the violin teacher phoned her, indicating that although all the violin places were full, there was availability in keyboard instruction and that this would give him a good musical foundation for later learning the violin. The mother asked whether Jason (who was now starting school) could also take keyboard lessons, and both sons were admitted. Jason said that it was his mother's decision for him to start lessons in keyboard performance, and that he was glad she had made this choice.

Jason has now been taking keyboard instruction since the previous year. These classes take place once a week on Wednesdays, at the school. When I ask what he does in keyboard lessons, Jason explains that they are given a little book and have to play out of it. "If we make mistakes, then we start all over again." He said he likes the book because it has "nice songs." Jason says that the teacher reads books and says what you have to do and sometimes she plays music for him. He thinks he's "kind of good" at the keyboard. Jason's mother reminds him that he played in the Eisteddfod. This is a public event at which students perform before adjudicators. He remembers about this and tells me that the Eisteddfod took place at his school and he played at the front of the hall, just below the stage. I ask him how he feels when he plays and he says it feels "nice."

Jason participates in the school choir, with rehearsals twice a week, Tuesdays early morning and Fridays after break. He enjoys how they learn different songs and says it's a "fun feeling" to sing in the choir. He likes the "Angels" song,[4] but does not remember how to sing it at this moment. He tells me that the teacher sometimes plays the piano while they sing, and other times they play the drums. In addition to being in the choir, Jason describes how his school class has a weekly music lesson with the same music teacher who teaches choir.

Jason's mother explains that "his first love is the drums; he would love to do the drums . . . his heart is there."

Descriptions of Family Musical Activities

Jason speaks fondly about how they all sing together in the evenings with his Dad playing guitar. His Mom likes to sing with them, too. Jason's grandfather plays keyboard by ear and they love to hear him play when he visits. Each year at Christmastime, Jason's uncle and family come down on holiday from Johannesburg, bringing instruments with them. The family music making during the festive season is obviously a highlight of this time, with everyone participating with great joy.

I ask Jason if he and his Dad ever play their instruments together—he at the keyboard and his Dad on the guitar. He says they did once, not playing from the book, but a song his Dad "knows how to play" and he was singing at the same time.

Jason explains that the family listens to music on the radio whenever they are in the car together. First, they pray, and then they listen to the radio all the way to school. Jason describes their prayer as "praise, thank, and ask." Sometimes he sings along to the radio; sometimes he sits quietly and listens; and sometimes they talk a little bit.

Jason listens to music on the TV with his brother early on Saturday mornings, while his parents are still sleeping. There are three programs, one after the other, which he describes as having music at the start and end.

Enkosi, the Second Participant

Enkosi (Figure 8.2) is a seven-year-old boy who attends the same school as Jason. His parents are both well qualified and highly skilled. The mother is a technical

Figure 8.2. Picture of Enkosi in South Africa. Published with parental permission.

operator, having studied electrical engineering, and the father is an operator, having studied in the field of chemistry. Enkosi has a brother of eleven years old and a sister age four. They live in a middle-class neighborhood, outside of the residential feeder area for the school he attends,[5] but within the same city municipality. Their visually appealing, freestanding brick house is surrounded by a well-maintained garden with grass, foliage, and parking areas for the cars. Security features include a high metal fence and electric gates. I was welcomed in and shown around several bedrooms, the kitchen and bathroom, dining room and living room. The entire family sits with Enkosi and me during the full interview, listening enthusiastically.

Sources of Musical Stimulation in the Home

The family sings church music in the home every evening. Enkosi's brother takes lessons on the keyboard and his mother says that she encourages him to practice every night, but he definitely practices on Monday and Wednesday nights in preparation for his lessons. Enkosi explains proudly that "My brother taught me how to do the scale with one hand and I practice a lot and I do it perfect." Enkosi demonstrates the fingering of the scale on the table where he is sitting. "The first time it does go wrong. But then I done it. . . . Often not perfectly, like my brother did his fingers on there. I did it, and then he let me go, and I tried it . . . I got it right . . . I asked my dad a lot. My dad said *yes* a lot. Then I tried to do it and I tried to do it and I tried to do it and then I got to it." Enkosi looked up at me, beaming with satisfaction. The family members escort me from the dining room, through the lounge and down the passage to a smaller room where everyone gathers around the keyboard. Enkosi stands in front of the keyboard and shows me how he plays the C-major scale ascending and descending, which he does masterfully with his right hand. His sister watches with rapt attention at one end of the keyboard, gives two huge nods of the head when he is finished, and starts clapping excitedly. I can see on Enkosi's face that he is pleased with his performance.

Enkosi's brother then demonstrates one of his pieces, first collecting his music book from another room. He balances the book on top of the keyboard, opens it, and leans it against the wall. He is standing with a hand on the keyboard, and hesitates for quite a while. I suggest he might like to fetch a chair. He seems happy to do that and sits waiting to begin. The parents encourage him by saying that Enkosi will sing. The brother then begins playing the keyboard, reading the notation in the book. He plays the entire theme song from the film *Titanic*, with the melody in the right hand and a simplified bass line in the left hand. Enkosi is standing close by, avidly watching the hands on the keyboard and singing the lyrics intently. He knows all the words. He sings accurately on pitch, with a clear voice. His sister watches him play, moving her arms to the song, as though conducting or doing rhythmic actions, and she is doing her best to mouth the words as well.

Parental Musical Background

Both Enkosi's parents have very active musical backgrounds. Their culture is rich in singing, with everyone in the community participating. The family sings when they are with friends. They explain that there is no need for instruments or "back tracks" [backing tracks], as they sing in harmony. Instruments are only used now and again.

Church singing is another rich part of their cultural heritage. Enkosi's father had been very active in the Seventh-day Adventist church when he was growing up, whereas the mother was less actively involved, becoming more so when she married.

Enkosi's father is an active member of a large professional community choir called Voices of Cape Town that specializes in a unique style that blends traditional South African music with jazz, sometimes accompanied by an instrumental combo. He is proud to be in a choir that tours internationally, performing compositions and arrangements by the director, Lungile Jacobs.

Musical Instruments

Enkosi has access to a digital keyboard in the home, which is placed on a stand. They explain that they have no musical toys because when they get them, the children use them so much that they break.

Media Available in the Home

Enkosi is allowed to operate a radio in the living room, but he explains that you cannot choose the music: "the radio plays the music." The parents explain that they listen to only one radio station: Umhlobo Wenena, an isiXhosa-language radio station with a name meaning "a real friend." They listen to the Gospel music. Enkosi and the family also listen to audio cassettes at home. On Sundays, the parents allow them all to watch a regular weekly TV program that features choirs. Enkosi says that it makes him feel happy to watch the choirs. The family listens to the radio in the car going to school and church. Enkosi's mother stresses how much he loves listening to CDs in the car.

Favorite Repertoires

Enkosi tells me that he likes the songs from the play he mentions they will be doing at school the next week. "I can remember one," he says: "Hambo Lala."[6] He performs the song for me standing up, pointing his forefinger on the words "no noise" and doing rhythmic actions during the chorus of rocking a baby in his

Figure 8.3. Score for "Hambo Lala." Written and composed by Bettina Schouw. Courtesy of African Cream Music.

Figure 8.4. Score of opening phrase of "Seven, the Sabbath Day" (composer unknown).

Figure 8.5. Score of opening phrase of "Box Song" (composer unknown).

arms. The words *thula baba, hambo lala*, of the South African isiXhosa language means "hush, baby, go to sleep" (see Figure 8.3). The little sister moves her body rhythmically to Enkosi's singing and claps on the offbeat. Enkosi sings with a strong voice, without any hesitation, with good intonation and a vigorous rhythmic style in his movements. Enkosi repeats the last line twice, slowing down the beat. Once the song is over, Enkosi gives a wide, beaming smile and the entire family claps and exclaims vocally. I ask Enkosi what he feels when he is singing and he says, "I feel happy, because I like the actions."

The family discusses the singing they do together in the evenings before prayers. Enkosi likes one called "Seven, the Sabbath Day" (see Figure 8.4). He decides to demonstrate a finger action song, his fingers moving on the table.

The father suggests the "Box" song, which he knows Enkosi likes and all the children then stand up with their father to perform it together (see Figure 8.5). They do movements that mimic the words of the song. Each verse is repeated and they make three loud kissing sounds on both hands, raised up to their lips at that moment. When they refer to members of the family, or Jesus, they kiss their hands. But when they refer to the Devil, they frown seriously and punch the one hand on the other three times instead of kissing. There are peels of laughter from the whole family afterward. They experience a tangible joy from participation in this song.

Engagement in Organized Activities

The mother explains that her children grew up attending the Seventh-day Adventist church. The entire congregation participates in "praise worship" and she describes church music as "embedded in the children." From the youngest age, the children sing solo, in groups, and as a family in church services. Those who learn instruments at school play their instruments as "backup" to the church singing. In addition, children from birth to age fifteen attend "children's ministries" sessions where they learn their own praise and worship songs.

Enkosi also hears children playing instruments in school music classes and concerts. He does not yet take formal music lessons but says he likes the drum and flute. His father explains that, fortunately, at school, children can learn an instrument. Hearing of their older son's opportunity to learn keyboard at school, they purchased one. He says that their base will be the keyboard but that later they will have a chance to choose their own instruments. Enkosi sings in the school choir twice weekly. He announced that next week they are going to do a musical play—about a bug and Aladdin.

Descriptions of Family Musical Activities

The father explains that the focal point of music in the home is the nightly singing of church choruses, immediately prior to their prayer session. The whole family participates and, typically, they move as they sing, either rhythmically moving their bodies according to the beat of the music, or doing specific actions linked to the text of the songs. They listen to the radio together, both at home and in the car. On Sundays they listen together to choirs on TV.

Discussion: Lessons Learned

As I had expected from the outset of this study, my investigations presented me with an entirely different social scenario from the one in which I had been raised. In the days of the Apartheid regime, the two boys participating in the study would not have been living in these suburban locations, nor would they have had access to this particular school. Each of their parents had acquired a tertiary education that allowed them to procure professional jobs and enjoy middle-class lifestyles with their children. They were realizing the dreams of the freedom struggle.

The children both clearly love music passionately. They exude joy in musical experiences and show respect for musical processes, their instruments, and the media they use for listening. They demonstrate a high level of proficiency in singing and have strong voices, good rhythmic skill, and beautiful tone quality. Their music is socially based in the family, school, and community settings. Their lives are filled with daily regular active music making and listening activities.

Corroborating the conclusions of Tudge (2008), the interviews indicate that the musical lives of both children predominantly reflect the musical cultures of their parents. In both these cases, these are inextricably associated with the parents' religious affiliations. In each case, the religious faith of the parents appears to be the focal point around which they center the existence of the family. The parents of both children explained how the children had grown up in rich musical environments in their churches. Furthermore, they had infused their homes with this music, including a session of live family music making every evening. They worshipped and prayed in song, and one family included live instrumental accompaniment. When selecting favorite repertoires, both children mentioned songs from these family worship sources. The religious beliefs of these families did not surprise me, nor did the fervor of their devotion. While the country's constitution respects and protects all religions, it is evident that Christianity has a widespread and devoted following, crossing white, black, and colored populations (Thompson, 1999). The country's first black president, Nelson Mandela, addressed the 1999 Parliament of the World's Religions, acknowledging traditional African religions for their contributions to humanity's spiritual heritage, and the broad range of religions engaged in the freedom struggle, adding: "Without the church, without religious institutions, I would never have been here today." As described by Loots (1997), the children's music is "the voice" of their culture, "the narrative of its poetry, ideologies, beliefs, and lifestyles" (p. 279). Their music and the proud, elated ways in which they share it speak volumes about these children's religious beliefs, their ideals, their values, and their lifestyles.

The Universal Declaration of Human Rights (1948, Article 26) states that "Parents have a prior right to choose the kind of education that shall be given to their children," a sentiment that was publicly endorsed by Mandela. Under the South African Constitution, children have the right to education. While schools typically serve children from their local neighborhoods, parents are able to apply for their children to attend schools outside their residential areas. The choices made by the parents on the schooling of their children has a powerful influence on the boys' musical identities, corresponding to Tudge's theory (2008). Both families had sent applications to the school, even though their homes were outside of the school's immediate neighborhood, and the boys had been accepted.

Besides the fact that each of the students receives weekly class music education from a qualified music specialist, both parents had encouraged their sons to participate in twice-weekly choir rehearsals and had also submitted formal applications for school instrumental instruction. One of the boys had been accepted into weekly keyboard classes and the other was learning from his older brother who had been accepted. As a result, both families had keyboard instruments in the home and encouraged their sons to practice daily. When asked to demonstrate their home musical activities, both boys had swiftly mentioned their keyboard playing and eagerly demonstrated it. Although keyboard may not have been the families' first choice and the teachers had offered this with the option of later moving to another instrument, the parent's applications to the school nevertheless directly led to this opportunity. This finding supports the view that the choices of the parents regarding the settings in which they place they children influence the children's development (Tudge, 2008). I was interested to see that the piano method book used in the school tuition and home practice does not seem to have strayed far from the one I had been given at the age of seven in the mid-1960s. It centers on middle C and teaches the child to play individual notes one hand at a time, through a literacy-based approach.

The two children whom I interviewed enjoy very different media for engaging in musical activities than what I had known. This is somewhat expected, due to the commodification of music in childhood (Bickford, 2011, 2012; Young, 2009). During most of my childhood, public television was not available in South Africa and the gramophone in my family's lounge was the center for listening to music on the radio or on 45 rpm and LP records. The music I heard represented a range of Western musical traditions: classical, light classics, traditional Scottish music, musicals, jazz, and popular music. These boys have access to television, CD/DVD players, and car radios. In both families, the music to which they are exposed through these media includes mostly music associated with their religions, and in Enkosi's family, specifically choral music. While Enkosi plays music cassettes, Jason uses multiple additional devices such as iPads and Wii games.

I was able to confirm the school's maintenance of the excellent music program for which it has continued to be well known since my childhood days. I also learned of a major expansion from focused piano, theory, and choral instruction to a wide range of instrumental tuition and ensemble opportunities, including Junior String Ensemble; Senior String Ensemble; Wind Band; Brass Band; Recorder Ensemble; Percussion Group (including African percussion) and School Orchestra. With these diverse options, the musical life of a South African child attending this school today can be very different from what was characteristic during my early childhood. I further noticed that when selecting their favorite songs for demonstration, both boys identified songs from their school choir, showing how much they love the repertoire associated with it. I noticed how these songs differ from those we studied in my school days, which at the time mostly represented Western folk, classical, and church hymn traditions, or songs from British and American musicals, such as *Oliver* and *The Sound of Music*. The boys' school songs identified here appear to have roots in popular music, jazz, and/or ethnic traditions. For example, "Angels" and "Boogie Bugs "have influences from British and American popular music cultures, and "Hambo Lala" includes traditional South African isiXhosa influences. The examples of school choral music reflect a diversity of musical content beyond anything I had experienced in school music activities. The increasing diversity in South African school music curricula has been long promoted in the prophetic urgings of leaders in the music education profession (Heunis, 1993; Lucia, 1992; Magubane, 1998; Oehrle, 1988; van Tonder, 1992; Woodward, 1994). Admittedly, this is a far more privileged school than most schools in South Africa, and the rich musical curriculum is indicative of long and generous financial and cultural infusions into the school throughout its history. However, it is also the outworking of teachers and administrators who value the arts and continue to place them high on the list of priorities for children's development. And behind these are the educational policies that Woodward (2007, p. 40) exhorts are "needed to protect children's voices and to ensure not only that their musical heritage is nourished and their artistic creativity fostered but also that we seek out and listen to what they say through their music."

There was evidence of ethnic roots in some of Enkosi's musical worlds, although there was no specific interest shown in ethnic instruments by either child. This is not surprising, considering the predominance of Western instruments heard live or via various technological media in their home, school, and religious settings, a phenomenon that is likely typical of the culture of many urban children in South Africa. These boys appear to be less exposed to traditional ethnic instrumental music, apart from the African marimbas and *djembes* that are commonly available in percussion ensembles in local schools. Jason's listening and music-making world includes predominantly instruments of Western origin, while Enkosi's musical culture is rooted in harmonic choral music that is characteristically unaccompanied. Although it has strong Western influences, this music is distinct from typical Western hymnody and often has strong ethnic rhythmic, harmonic, and melodic characteristics.

Conclusions

Music educators worldwide who speak out for change might be encouraged by the transformation in curricular direction that took place in South African education in the years that followed strong urging from its own academic leaders in the music field. School teachers might also be encouraged in their efforts to promote lifelong musical enjoyment, seeing anecdotal examples here of school music being shared by children in their homes with entire families. In light of many such studies, parents can know that their choices in home, school, and community settings have a powerful influence on their children's musical cultures, attitudes, values, and lifestyles. Students can be empowered by the examples of South African children peacefully protesting an oppressive government and triumphing in achieving democratic freedoms and the recognition of human rights for all. Interviewing these two children and their families afforded me the enormous privilege of being invited briefly into the homes and lives of these two delightful young children. I deeply appreciated the warmth and willingness to engage with me, extended by them and their family members. I was able to celebrate the observable changes in a society that had come about through decades of political struggle, allowing children of all races to learn side-by-side in schools and to live together in unrestricted neighborhoods. I thought nostalgically back to our youthful days of the freedom struggle, which had played a part in the evolution of this joyful outcome.

Notes

1. *Toyi-toying* is a highly rhythmic style of dancing characteristic of peaceful protests in South Africa.

2. The *Supernatural* DVD (2006) is the third live worship album produced by Hillsong Kids. Hillsong Kids is the children's ministry of Hillsong Church, a Pentecostal megachurch that originated in Sydney, Australia.

3. This is part of the school's musical production of *Aladdin*, based on the Disney version, but adapted to accommodate all the students. Hence the inclusion of "Boogie Bugs," written and composed by Ann Bryant, which was to be sung by the bugs in Aladdin's cave. The score is published by Faber Music in *Teaching Foundation Music*, with audio CD.

4. Pop song by Robbie Williams and Guy Chambers, voted 2005 Special BRITs 25 Award for the best single from the past twenty-five years, by Brit Awards.

5. The school generally accepts students from within a close geographical neighborhood surrounding the school, but takes a relatively small number from outside the area.

6. A song written and composed by South African musician Bettina Schouw. She performs it on the CD *The Goodnight Songs* published by African Cream Music, 2008, in a lower key than the one sung by Enkosi.

9 The Influence of Parental Goals and Practices on Children's Musical Interests and Development

A Perspective on Chinese Families in Singapore

Chee-Hoo Lum

A man who is not good, what can he have to do with music?
Confucius, *Analects*

Being an avid music lover, the father of eight-year-old Elvi used this Confucius saying from *Sishu Wujing* (Four books and five classics) written before 300 BCE, as justification for why he feels music should be cultivated in his child so that she can grow up to be a good person; a person who is cultured, resilient, and developed with the right moral values. Parents in Chinese Singaporean families often acknowledge, as does Elvi's father, that "childhood is a much-treasured part of the life process within the Chinese family and as the child grows and develops, he or she should be carefully guided by parents and the community to successfully *chen ren* [become adults]" (Lum and Whiteman, 2012, p.2). Chinese parents "have profound admiration for the potential of children's intellectual and moral capabilities, which must be realized through education and development" (Kinney, 1995, p.12). Clearly, Elvi's father has basic beliefs about how he wants to raise his child and what he wants her to achieve through the learning of music.

This chapter will provide a particular Southeast-Asian perspective, specifically, a Singaporean perspective on the role of parents in influencing children's musical interests and development. Sociocultural factors abound in terms of home influences that can affect a child's musical development, and include siblings, relatives, technology, and social media. This investigation aims to flesh out the role of parental goals and practices in children's musical practices, to provide a glimpse among a plethora of other confounding factors within the home environment. The guiding questions include: (1) What are parental goals in children's musical practices? (2) What are parental practices in achieving these goals? and (3) What is contextually significant about the Singaporean situation in terms of the role of parents in the musical practices of children? Also, in line with the MyPlace, MyMusic project (Young, 2012b), the researcher, investigating guiding question (3), is eager to "collect information on any musical traditions (with particular attention to any traditions associated with religious practices) which may impact on the range and nature of musical practice for young children in the home" (Young, 2012b, p. 6). The MyPlace, MyMusic data, which comprised interviews with parents done by the collaborative researchers in the United Kingdom, Spain, Kenya, Denmark, Taiwan, Brazil, the United States, the Netherlands, Italy, Greece, South Africa, and Israel, provided a glimpse of how parents in some of these countries were involved in shaping their children's musical practices. An analysis of the MyPlace, MyMusic data based on the guiding questions in this research study yielded some initial thoughts on the subject. The intention in this follow-on study, however, is not to make a comparison between countries but to use the MyPlace, MyMusic data and the themes it revealed as starting points of consideration and analysis with the current research data sets.

McPherson (2009) in suggesting a framework for studying parent–child interactions stated that "only a handful of studies have examined the role of parents in children's musical development" (p. 90). This research study thus also takes up McPherson's call to add to existing literature on the topic, with a specific focus on parental goals and practices in the context of Chinese families in Singapore. Parental goals in this study are defined as the values, beliefs, attitudes, and aspirations held by parents in shaping the specific goals they hold for their children (Spera, 2006; Wentzel, 1998), and parental practice that focuses on the "specific behaviors used (by parents) to socialize children" (McPherson, 2009, p. 93).

Methodology

As part of a modular assignment requirement for an elementary music methods course to help preservice teachers in Singapore better understand the role of music in children's daily lives, first, the preservice teachers were all tasked with locating a child they might know, between six and twelve years old. This could be their own child or a child of their relatives and friends. Second, they were tasked to set up a single meeting with the child and his/her parents at their home, to interview the parents and the child, and follow the investigation guidelines adapted from the MyPlace, MyMusic protocol (Young, 2012).

Eventually, after examining and analyzing the data, each teacher was tasked with writing out and submitting a three- to four-thousand–word narrative based

Table 9.1. Information on child participants in Singapore.

Child	Ethnicity	Gender	Age	Religious affiliation	Socioeconomic status	Instrument(s) currently learning in formal lessons
1	Chinese	M	6	Buddhist	High	Piano
2	Chinese	M	7	Christian	Middle	Piano
3	Chinese	M	7	Christian	Middle	Piano
4	Chinese	F	8	Christian	High	Piano
5	Chinese	F	8	—	Middle	Piano, violin, Electone
6	Chinese	M	9	Christian	High	Piano and violin
7	Chinese	F	9	Christian	Middle	Piano
8	Chinese	F	9	Christian	High	Piano
9	Chinese	M	10	Christian	Middle	Violin and drums
10	Chinese	M	10	—	Middle	Piano (stopped)
11	Chinese	F	11	—	High	Piano
12	Chinese	M	11	Christian	High	Piano (stopped)
13	Chinese	F	11	Buddhist	Middle	Piano
14	Chinese	F	11	—	High	Piano
15	Chinese	M	11	—	Middle	—
16	Chinese	F	12	Christian	High	Piano

on everyday musical experiences in the child's home. The name of the child and family remained anonymous in the narrative.

There was no specific requirement that the preservice teachers select a child of particular ethnicity, gender, or inclination toward particular musical practices. The preservice teachers were free to decide whom they felt might be a suitable participant for the project. Figure 9.1 shows the basic information about each child:

All sixteen children are Chinese, ages six to twelve. There are eight boys and eight girls. All belong to middle to high socioeconomic status (SES) families and twelve of the sixteen children are currently learning piano. Nine belong to the Christian faith and two are from Buddhist families (the religious affiliation of five families was not specified). Also, in nine families, one or both parents can play one instrument (mainly piano) or more, and four mothers in this group of sixteen are public school music teachers.

After gaining written consent from this class of sixteen preservice teachers (all of whom happen to be of Chinese ethnicity) to use the content of their narrative as data points, this researcher amassed the sixteen narratives and process-coded the data (Saldaña, 2010) in terms of parental goals and practices. Some codes that emerged include: Influence of musical repertoire, Influence of religion, Enjoyment, Relaxation, Discipline, Academic focus, Starting at young age, and Support and encouragement. The data were then chunked and analyzed in detail in analytical memos that were written before establishing the findings. The researcher was also eager to locate in the analysis contextually significant content in the narratives that spoke to a localized Singaporean understanding of the phenomenon.

The codes bore some similarities to the MyPlace, MyMusic data (e.g., Ilari, chapter 6, this volume; Koutsoupidou, chapter 5, this volume). "Enjoyment" for instance, emerged from the MyPlace, MyMusic data, with parents wanting their child or children to take up an instrument or engage in musical activities as a form of enjoyment, as a healthy pursuit that also helps in social, family bonding and community building. The MyPlace, MyMusic data also included some parents who spoke about how they were not given a chance to learn an instrument when they were younger and hoped that their child would be able to take up an instrument if he or she wants to. Other parents described influences from religion or how they discovered particular musical talents in their child, as the reason they want to provide formal music lessons so as to further the child's interest. There were also enlightened opinions from parents about how music would bring their child closer to their own culture and how the development of a keen ear through music might allow their child to be cognizant and sensitive to the sound worlds around them, and to understand various functions and uses of music. Interestingly, the Taiwanese parents (Chinese) included in the MyPlace, MyMusic data mentioned how learning music would help their child to increase concentration and focus, and to develop the cultivation of "elegance" "peace and quietness." This particular finding resonated with the data that emerged in the opinions of the Chinese Singaporean parents in this study as well.

Findings

Enjoyment, Relaxation, De-stressing, and Family Bonding

High-stakes assessment is "the gateway to each level of education" in Singapore. According to Gregory and Clarke (2003, p. 71), "The Singaporean education system is intensely competitive. Only a small percentage of students are selected for the top stream in the education system, and an even smaller percentage make it into Singapore's university education system." It is no wonder that one of the frequent goals some parents stated for wanting their children to be engaged in musical learning is so that they can find an avenue, an outlet to enjoy, relax, and de-stress themselves from their academic work. As a mother articulated, "Given the kind of stressful environment that children are going through nowadays, I think it's an avenue for them to have some sort of stress release. My objective of letting them learn is so that they will be able to play." There is also a sense from some parents who play musical instruments themselves that music is used for family bonding purposes, stating that,

> [We] believe in modeling the love of music to our children. We play music together as a family;
> [We] believe that music not only helps to create fun and joy between the child and parents, but also increases family bonding; and
> During free time, the family will get together at the piano and we will sing Chinese and English classics while [mother] plays the piano. [Father] will play along on the ukulele.

Music Serving Religious Purposes

Interestingly, the sets of parents who spoke of using music as family bonding were also among the nine sets of parents in the Christian families who stated that one of their key purposes in involving their children in music making is so that at some point in their lives they might be able to use the musical skills they have developed to serve in the music ministry of their church, to be able to play as accompanists in church services, or be part of the local church's Christian Contemporary Music (CCM) groups. "CCM involves the pairing of a Gospel message or Christian worldview with popular forms of rock music . . . a representative of a large Christian subculture" (Howard, 1992, pp. 123–124), which is a growing phenomenon in local churches in Singapore. Parents spoke confidently about this:

> [My children] reaped the rewards of their labor (hours of practicing on the piano) as they get to play in school ensembles and church ensembles, as well as for fellowship group meetings, children worship services and weddings in church.
>
> Family involvement in church leads to [my child] liking to hum worship songs and hymns. To the family, singing worship songs in church or in private is one of the many ways we express ourselves to God. In the daytime, Christian music can often be heard playing in the background (from CDs of Christian music being played at home). [My child] was exposed to music also because of the possibility that he might be able to service in the music ministry in church in the future.

These similar sets of parents also spoke of their concern about popular music in the media. There seems to be a moral high ground: some parents denounce the influences of some popular music repertoire. As Howard (1992) articulated, "Religion and rock music have long had a love/hate relationship. Rock music is often charged with being a perverter of America's youth and an underminer of Christian moral values" (p. 123). These parents were

> particularly concerned that [my child] does not make informed decisions and prefer[s] popular music just because of peer influence, social media, etc. We are concerned that schools might use any form of popular music too quickly or solely, such that [my child] is not focusing on the musical aspects but rather, picking up other values such as the fame, glamour, materialism, etc. We would like to see [my child] being exposed to a wide range of music, not just popular music.
>
> I need to look at the lyrics of the song, because I'm quite particular about it. I need to know the content but I haven't had time to go through the songs. If it's not appropriate, I will tell [my child] not to listen. I am concerned that if [my child] starts listening and singing the inappropriate lyrics of some songs, [my child] may get the wrong impression that would be difficult to reverse.

The musical idiom in which CCM functions is essentially the popular music genre but presumably because the lyrical content stems from a Christian worldview, the parents did not raise any objections. Music thus serves as lived and living practice for these families and their children, having significance in their family and spiritual life. And because the nature of the religious music services in these local churches functions within a Western classical and popular music idiom using instruments like the piano, keyboard, guitar, and drums, it would seem natural for these parents to align and sign their children up for formal music lessons at home that emphasize these particular instruments within a similar music paradigm.

Perseverance and Discipline

Some parents had strong beliefs that allowing their children to formally learn a musical instrument and establish a routine of practicing and performing on the instrument is a way to develop and prepare them for life skills like perseverance and discipline. As they remarked:

> When they are young, they actually have a lot of free time. They have enough free time, so they can actually do more when they are younger. Not so much to stress them out, but it's also part of training of discipline.
>
> The children learnt to put in effort when they had to repeat difficult passages, bring the playing up to speed, and adjusting the tuning of each note. They also learn to focus on something that they need to do which translated into their revision of their academic studies.
>
> After going through one year of lessons with [my child], I find that music instills discipline, coordination skills and multi-tasking skills (having to read notes, play the piano, and step on the pedal).

Our Colonial Legacy

All the children mentioned in the quotes above have private music lessons on the piano or the violin, learning essentially a Western classical music repertoire. As

Kok (2006) accurately surmised from Singapore's colonial past, "In Malaysia (and Singapore), the piano had graced the homes of expatriates and the wealthy since the British arrived. An unmistakable aura surrounded the instrument; it represented, to the Malaysian (Singaporean) mind, qualities associated with the colonizers' lifestyle: 'cultured,' 'wealthy,' 'powerful,' 'well-educated,' and 'refined.' Privileged were those who played it" (Kok, 2006, p. 93).

While three of the sixteen children are currently not taking any private music lessons, all but one has had formal music lessons in the past. While some did not have the discipline to persevere, fifteen of the sixteen children in this set of narratives have all been enrolled by their parents at some point to take graded examinations with the Associated Board of the Royal Schools of Music (ABRSM) and thus their musical associations with Western classical art music. According to Lum and Dairianathan:

> ABRSM had local representation in Singapore as early as 1948 and enrollment for this music examinations body has grown ever since, now totaling at least forty thousand students a year with total annual revenue of eight million Singapore dollars. During the "examination season", all music studios at many private music centers would be fully booked with students practicing and rehearsing their set pieces and piano teachers checking on the conditions of the pianos while parents hovered protectively around the studio spaces. (Lum and Dairianathan, 2013, p. 336)

Some parents seem to quantitatively equate their child's progression in musical development with the graded ABRSM qualifications, stating:

> I expect [my child] to pass her ABRSM exams as it's quite expensive to retake.
> [My child] has a natural flair for music and is an intelligent child.
> Practices her piano often. I hope for [my child] to attain Grade 8.

The child also absorbed this "obsession" to complete the graded levels: "I am so happy to get distinction for all my exams, I want to get distinction!"

Perhaps it is the structure that ABRSM has set up that allows these parents (in confirming their beliefs in and manifestation of practices) to see clearly and physically how their child is able to play increasingly difficult pieces in each ascending grade, a "religious reliance on what the ABRSM symbolized as 'homogeneity of habitus' together with officializing strategies which imposed ABRSM certification as evidence of competence" (Lum and Dairianthan, 2013, p. 336). It is perhaps also the "illusion of the elite" from our colonial legacy, in unquestioningly trusting the status of Western classical art music. As one mother puts it, "I believe that people who are more musically inclined [with reference to a taste toward Western classical art music] are more *atas* [a Malay word for high class], romantic, charming and know how to enjoy life and I hope that [my child] would have these traits."

Returning to Confucius

Reiterating Confucius, "A man who is not good, what can he have to do with music?" (2001, p. 86), there seems to be an underlying ethos rooted in Confucius in the thinking of goals and practices of these Singaporean Chinese parents' toward the musical practices of their children. This ethos seemed to resonate with Kok's interpretation:

> As the piano requires much discipline and time to master, the enterprise of learning the instrument is in line with Confucian teachings, which emphasize among other things continuous, in-depth, and committed efforts in all educational undertakings. Confucius had also taught that cultivation of music would lead to "goodness" of character. Thus a Chinese child's successful mastery of music and the piano would engender satisfaction and guarantee respect for the family from within as well as outside of the Chinese community. (Kok, 2006, p. 93)

One could also conjecture that the parents' goals and practices linked to religious activities—such as the hope that their children will eventually play in church ministries, or even linked to Buddhism classes where one child, for instance, was encouraged to "perform singing and dancing fortnightly at the temple"—has an underlying ethos linked to Confucius's call for the musical development of the child that is aimed toward the child's becoming a "good person." Thus the "Chineseness" (linked to Confucian ethos and values) in these Singaporean families is perhaps more deeply rooted than appears at first glance. To move this conjecture forward, the researcher will have to probe more deeply on this issue with the parents concerned.

The Economic Impulse

Running through the minds of most of these sixteen sets of parents is a consistent belief that only by doing well in high-stakes assessments in Singapore (which does not translate to nonexaminable primary school subjects like the arts), can their child's career path be better guarded. There is a general consensus among this group of parents that their child's future economic survival should take priority. There is no shortage of convictions from a majority of parents about this firm belief:

> [My child's] academic studies are more important, especially in Singapore. We feel that having a good education is important in order to survive in this competitive society. We would always stress that [the child] completes her homework before she can play on the piano.
>
> [My child's] academic milestones carried precedence over his other activities. I removed all forms of recreational activity and focused very strongly on [my child's] preparation for national exams.

> It's not that we don't want them to enjoy themselves or [that we want to] restrict them from trying new things. It's just that if they are struggling to cope with their schoolwork, that's what we need to look at first. It's about priorities. At the end of the day, it's the grades that are going to get them into a good school and give them a good job.

Even gender bias comes clearly to the fore: "I reckon music is an extra and good skill to have. While I allow [my daughter] to become a musician in the future, I will not allow the more academically-inclined [my son] to take up any other career than being a doctor. It was a promise to his late grandfather that he would be a doctor." Perhaps the economic impulse that the Singapore government has long ingrained into the hearts and minds of Singaporeans has indeed taken root. As Navera (2013) stated, "The story of Singapore may be seen as a continuous struggle to thrive economically, first in a region wrought by years of colonial rule, then in an economic order where competitiveness appears to be a prime virtue" (p.4). The views of these parents seem to run in parallel with Singapore's cultural policy since the 1980s, represented by the government's economic attitude toward the arts, "That the arts can generate economic spin-offs is evident in the prioritization of urban regeneration, preservation of historic building, and the creation of arts zones—all of which are pursued to boost arts tourism in Singapore. . . . This rather pragmatic take on the arts relegates to the sidelines the humanistic perspective in which the arts are viewed as vital to the holistic development of the human person" (Navera, 2013, p. 14). A tension exists in the goals and practices of these parents toward their children's musical development, a balance that is tipped toward the economic impulse despite acknowledging all that music (or the arts) can bring for the child.

There are glimmers of hope though, as some parents noted:

> [My child's] academic subjects have improved ever since she took up
> piano lessons. . . . Piano lessons helped [my child] to focus better, especially [in] Mathematics.
>
> It is important that children are given opportunities to be exposed to both academics and the arts, and we believe in letting children engage in activities that interest them.
>
> We believe that the arts is a way to [spark children's] curiosity and open their minds.

But perhaps the most heartening of all remarks came from Elvi's mother who elegantly remarked, "We may not be able to know and plan what our future generation will and can achieve, but starting early with comprehensive music exposure, we can be sure that our children will grow up with enthusiasm and joy to tread upon the road ahead confidently."

Conclusions

Parents play an influential role in many decision processes based on their values and beliefs that can affect the musical development of their children. The analysis of the sixteen narratives has resulted in some contextually significant observations. It seems that most of the Singaporean parents from these middle- to high-SES families want to provide their children with formal music lessons starting at a young age. They were quite specific about the particular type of musical genre that they wanted their child to experience and learn through these formal lessons—that of the Western classical art tradition—and through the route of graded examinations from the ABRSM. More often than not, the instrument of choice was the piano. The parents were, however, not opposed to their children's listening and experiencing other kinds of music at home, as long as these were not popular songs containing what the parents would consider inappropriate lyrical content.

The drive toward such parental practice to guide their children in their musical development seems to be governed by these parents' beliefs that having these musical skill sets will enable their children: (1) to cope and balance out the stresses in their academic life, as an outlet for enjoyment, relaxation, and de-stressing; (2) to come together with the family as a social bonding activity, to make music as a family; (3) to socialize with their friends through music but, more significantly, to be able to play in religious activities, as a way to glorify and strengthen their faith; and (4) to develop perseverance and discipline through the practice of the musical instrument, an idea stemming from the larger belief that these are traits that will lead their child to develop into a "good" person and successfully *chen ren* [become adults]. Underlying these parental goals/beliefs, however, is a more pragmatic stance, where music is still seen as an "additional thing to have," if, and only if, their children can do well in their academic studies, which is assumed to be tied to their future economic survival and success.

Having carried out this analysis, this researcher is interested in probing into the psyche of more Chinese families in Singapore, to determine whether the Confucian ethos of music education as a way forward to the development of "good" moral values is indeed a concept that is being played out through the provision of formal music lessons for their children. And if so, are these parental practices always followed through? Furthermore, are there particular musical genres (in this instance, the lure of the Western classical art tradition due to our colonial baggage) that seem to fit well into this ethos (clearly, the structure of the graded examinations of the ABRSM and the tangible paper qualifications seem to be good, visible indicators for this current set of parents).

As a music educator interested in issues of diversity and inclusion, cognizant of the many musics that surround us and the varied musical, social, historical, and cultural gems and ideas that can be shared with students, alarm bells are sounding despite knowing that this research narrative is based on a small biased sampling of the Singaporean population. Could it be true as Huang (2012) suggests, that "the transcultural power of Western classical music is felt by many Asians . . . who have become passionately devoted to an art form that is far removed in time and place from the 'authentic' music defined by their indigenous traditional cultures?" (p. 172) If so, and if Singaporean parents are among the key players responsible for the propagation of this phenomenon, should local music educators start thinking hard about what they are teaching students in their general music classroom to expand their repertoire and musical worldview, and, reiterating the words of one parent, "to [spark children's] curiosity and open their minds?" Parents should perhaps take heed and be constantly reminded that,

> All modulations of sound take their rise from the mind of man; and music is the intercommunication of them in their relations and differences. (K'ung-fu Tzu [Confucius], The Li Chi 1885/2008, p. 57)

Conclusion

Lessons Learned

Beatriz Ilari, Susan Young, and Claudia Gluschankof

Some years ago, as a group of early childhood researchers was contemplating a picturesque view of the hills of Frascati, Italy, a research project titled "MyPlace MyMusic" came about. A few months (and many exchanged e-mail messages) later, data were collected from different corners of the world and shared through a wiki. Translated interviews, field notes, jottings, musical recordings, videos, photos, drawings, maps, and others were carefully examined and became the source material for the chapters that make up the current volume. Here, we aimed to bring forward some possible interpretations of the data collected in twelve different countries, with seventeen, middle-class, seven-year-olds and their family members. But we could not end this book without touching on some important points that emerged from engaging in this research enterprise. For the purpose of clarity, we have categorized them into two main areas: (1) issues in a collaborative, qualitative music research project with children; and (2) musical childhoods: global issues and local variations.

Issues in a Collaborative, Qualitative Music Research Project with Children

The Situated Nature of the Research Enterprise

We began this project with the goal of collecting case study data that centered on children's musicking (Small, 1998) in the home, framed by sociocultural theories and empirical work on children's everyday lives (Gillen and Cameron, 2010; Tudge, 2008), as well as previous research on music in everyday life of children and adults (DeNora, 2000; Turino, 2006; Young, 2008). In our search for knowledge, two main ideas guided our efforts. First, we conceptualized our work from a perspective that recognizes children's musicking as both generated by and generating the sociocultural context within which it is embedded. Second, we were oriented by a qualitative epistemology, or, from the notion that humans are meaning makers and that knowledge exists not inside a person or in the world, but in the intersections between them (see Matsunobu and Bresler, 2013). That is, we entered the field knowing that our data would rely on children and adults who were historically, culturally, ethnically, socially, and psychologically situated. Likewise, we had a clear understanding of our own "situatedness" as researchers (Matsunobu and Bresler, 2013).

Furthermore, and given the relatively slow pace of academic publishing as well as the rapidness in the development of goods from the technological and commercial worlds, we knew beforehand that some aspects of our data would be time-sensitive. For instance, we were aware that part of the repertoires that would be mentioned or sung by our participants along with toys, digital media, videos, and other gadgets that existed in each home would probably have been completely different had we visited the families only a few months earlier or later. This was not entirely problematic because we also shared the belief that childhood is uniquely situated, or a time of its own. In other words, childhood was viewed in terms of "being" and not "becoming" from the very beginning of the research enterprise. Therefore, even when individual researchers examined the data from a developmental perspective (e.g., Persellin, chapter 7, this volume), they acknowledged the importance of experience and meaning making "in the moment."

In addition, it was interesting to see that, while a wide range of theories was used to construct individual chapters, the latter shared a common epistemology and a basic theoretical framework and research paradigm. The researchers each had a framework that served as a starting point for their work. Yet they were also free to follow any clues they deemed necessary and move with their work in any given direction. Consequently, each researcher adopted different strategies when interviewing children and adults. Furthermore, individual researchers also proposed varied interpretations of the data based on their own experiences, expertise, and perceptions. This could be interpreted as an additional layer of "situatedness" in this qualitative research project. We would also suggest that for any international collaborative project that brings together colleagues in different countries and different academic systems, with variations in their research cultures, it is important to allow for individual freedom within a common unifying structure.

Another noteworthy aspect was how rich and interesting our data were. As Matsunobu and Bresler (2013) would probably agree, the richness of the data that were collected afforded many possibilities of interpretation, which were then transformed into individual chapters. Unsurprisingly, while some researchers relied on the musical data, that is, sung renditions, invented songs, and performances during the "show and tell" (e.g., Andang'o and Pacheco; Gluschankof), others focused heavily on interviews (e.g., Koutsoupidou) or on narrative ways of knowing (e.g., Woodward) to create their works. Still others infused a longitudinal component to the data (e.g., Persellin) or went on to develop new ideas and studies from this project (e.g., Lum). From a methodological perspective, then, many levels of situatedness overlapped during the course of the entire research enterprise.

On Interviews, Data Analysis, and Interpretation

As discussed in the opening chapter, each researcher/fieldworker interviewed one or two children from her/his own ethnicity, cultural group, and social class. A common protocol was used and researchers and fieldworkers had some freedom to adapt it to their culture, the child, and the context. In Italy, for example, the fieldworker—a graduate student supervised by her tutor (who was not present during the stage of data collection)—visited the boy's house four times, and the girl's house twice, in order to build rapport with the children. Yet, in other countries this did not happen. Why did other fieldworkers not do the same? For some it was because they were following the protocol in a strict way. For others it was because the researchers were previously acquainted with the children (e.g., Spain, Brazil). This variability could equally be explained based on differences in fieldworkers' experiences with qualitative research. While all of the above could hold true, it was clear that the interviews were markedly different.

Parental attitudes also influenced the ways in which the interviews were conducted. In some homes, parents were present during the interview with the child (e.g., Kenya, Denmark), and their presence either facilitated the interview process or was a hindrance. In other homes, parents stepped aside (e.g., Israel) or were nowhere to be seen (e.g., Giovanna in Brazil), in order to give the interviewee–interviewer dyad some space. We interpret these contrasting parental behaviors as by-products of parenting styles and beliefs regarding children's autonomy, and in particular, expectations regarding their behavior with nonfamily adults. For example, in some societies children are encouraged to refrain from talking to strangers (e.g., the United States), which may bring some challenges to face-to-face interactions with unfamiliar people. Yet in other societies such practices are still somewhat common, particularly in contexts where there is some form of parental or adult supervision (e.g., Brazil).

Children's ways of being in the world, that is, their personalities (e.g., extroverted, wanting to please others), the type of relationship/rapport developed with the researcher, cultural norms, and expectations of childhood, were also seen to influence the quality of the interviews. For example, while Sissi in Israel, Charlie in the UK, and Maria in Spain not only answered questions but volunteered more information, Christine in Singapore barely spoke, but willingly sang and played. Likewise, it was perhaps the desire to please the adults who were present during the interview (i.e., the researcher and his mother) that led Brad in the

United States to confidently sing songs belonging to the Kodály-focused music classes from school, and not to comply with his mother's request to sing the patriotic song "This Land Is Your Land," to which he could not remember the words. That is, sometimes children showed independence and agency, possibly because the researcher or fieldworker did not belong to the child's everyday contexts of family and school, and may have been perceived as the "incompetent adult" (Corsaro and Molinari, 2001). This is consistent with the interview held in Greece with Melina, who probably perceived the researcher as a "less threatening adult" (and even an ally), given her desire to sing a favorite soccer team anthem, which was immediately censored by her mother. Taken together, these differences in the interviews align with the notion that interviews are not "an expression of an interviewee's own 'authentic voice' " (Alldred and Burman, 2005, p. 181). Rather, their emergence is intricately related to "filters" such as the research and interview questions, the perceptions that participants have of the situation, personal beliefs and values, biographies as well as the "structural constraints they face" (ibid.).

Linguistic issues and the nature of data transcription are also worthy of commentary. All but one interview was conducted in the first language of the child and researcher/fieldworker. (The only exception was the Israeli researcher who was speaking in her second language.) Interview data were then transcribed and translated into English, the lingua franca of the project. Unsurprisingly, the transcription and translation of data point to a "double translation," which raises dilemmas and implies that there were multiple interpretations. For example, the ways in which a researcher transcribes an interview can vary. The researcher may include nonverbal information such as pauses, hesitations and laughter, different inflections and intonation in the spoken voice, and gestures. This nonverbal information can convey important meanings in the interview. There again, some researchers in our team chose to share the video recordings of the interviews through the wiki. Although the spoken language was not always understood, it was possible to get a glimpse of the children's body language and speech inflections, which are important components of any interview, but rather difficult to transcribe. As Lange and Mierendorff (2011) have suggested, children sometimes express more with their bodies than with spoken language.

The interview transcripts offered, then, only partial information. Furthermore, given that all interview transcripts were presented in English, new dilemmas arose, in that translation is already a form of interpretation. Should the translations be literal or should researchers also translate ideas and culture-specific practices and their meanings? When a child's use of language is not appropriate or is grammatically incorrect, should this be translated? All these decisions are relevant to the representation of children's voices (Alldred and Burman, 2005). It was interesting that, when analyzing data, research team members often asked one another to help them "hear" children's voices in the text.

As each researcher/fieldworker went into the field to interview children and families, they did so within their own constructions of childhood and music. Each of us, in turn, read and interpreted the translated—and therefore interpreted—data, within our own constructions of childhood and music. This is consistent with the notion that "the theoretical stance of the researcher and their orientation to the construction of meaning will fundamentally affect the way in which interview material is used in analysis" (Westcott and Littleton, 2005, p. 153)

Whereas these methodological issues and dilemmas could be seen as limitations, they are proof of the complexity inherent in researching children from different cultures by researchers from different cultures, backgrounds, and theoretical stances.

The Role of New Technologies

Researchers have long been involved in substantial international collaborative research projects, including the above mentioned works by Gillen and Cameron (2010) and Tudge (2008). But what was different about our project was the use of digital technologies to facilitate the communication between researchers living in distinct time zones. Initially inspired by the affordances of the social networking service MySpace, which was quite popular at the onset of our collaboration, we decided to name our project MyPlace, MyMusic—as both a celebration of this communication tool and a reminder of its potential.[1] While we did not use MySpace in our project, we attempted to create a similar experience with a wiki.

As explained in the opening chapter, the research team exchanged data and ideas through the wiki, in order to overcome geographic separation. The degree of familiarity of each individual researcher with technology, however, played a role in terms of the amount of interactions that took place. While all researchers did upload their materials following a proposed timeline, some were found to engage more often with one another through the wiki's chat room than others, who appeared to favor communication through e-mail. The wiki afforded different levels of engagement with the data, which, in some ways, is consistent with the discussion on researcher situatedness presented earlier.

Another important central and defining feature of our project was that the wiki not only enabled information sharing but also allowed for a richer means of triangulation of data between research team members. Triangulation is what grants rigor and trustworthiness to qualitative research (Creswell, 2011; Mathison, 1988). Approaches to triangulation are many, and often include triangulating by time, space, and person; by investigator, or by methodology (Mathison, 1988). By virtue of tradition, qualitative research in music education tends to be more of an individual effort, and in most cases, the first triangulation approach (i.e., time, space, and person) seems to be the most commonly used. Our project, however, not only demonstrated the importance of comparing multiple data sources and member checking but also reinforced the importance of investigator triangulation. Given that our data were collected in different parts of the world and made use of translations, it was essential for researchers to constantly check whether interpretations of data collected in countries other than their own were logical and culturally sensitive. This, in turn, reinforced the need for constant dialogue between research team members throughout the process—from the early stages of data collection to the actual evaluation of completed chapters at a later time.

Ethical Issues

Other interesting issues also emerged in the process of using a wiki to disseminate, share, and interpret data, including ethical issues pertaining to data ownership and children's agency. Although these questions were raised throughout the process, they were more prominent at two specific times in the research process: at an earlier stage when consent forms were elaborated, and at a later time when the actual data were being interpreted and disseminated in academic circles.

The understanding of ethical issues in research is far from being consensual across the globe (Ilari, 2009). Whereas some countries have strict policies concerning institutional review boards and the like (e.g., the United States, the UK), others do not, particularly in music research (e.g., Brazil). Therefore, each researcher had to adapt an "overarching" ethical approval document from the University of Exeter to their local realities. For some (e.g., the United States), this process was quite straightforward because their institutions were used to such documents and procedures. But for others this turned out to be rather problematic. In Brazil, for example, the researchers had to "jump through many hoops" to get consent forms approved because the researchers' university did not have an institutional review board at the time and some parents did not understand the need to sign documents. This raises some questions regarding ethical procedures in research collaborations that involve multiple countries. Given many differences in research traditions, epistemologies, and paradigms, a question that remains is "who becomes ultimately responsible, should problems arise in a country other than the one where the 'main' approval was granted?" Furthermore, should a foreign university be held responsible for ethical issues in a foreign country, when the research is being coordinated by one of its researchers? These questions are very difficult to answer but they are incredibly important for those interested in international collaborations that involve the collection of empirical data.

In terms of ownership, the research team agreed that the data belonged first to their children/families, who received a copy of everything that was collected from individual research team members. Next, the group understood that their role was to give a voice to individual children and their families. As some type of "trustees" of individual and the collective group of children, the research team members could interpret and reinterpret the data as they wish, yet being careful to reference the entire project and team when presenting or publishing papers (e.g., Ilari, 2013b; Young, 2012b). After serving its main purpose (i.e., data dissemination and sharing among a specific research team), the wiki was disassembled and is no longer available or working.

Yet the question regarding children's autonomy in the research project as a whole remains. As in the "A Day in the Life" project (Gillen and Cameron, 2010), we questioned ourselves about the ways in which children will interpret their own participation (and our interpretations) in the years to come. When this book is finally published the children will be several years older and may view their participation—and this publication—very differently. Is there an ethical dilemma here, too, and should one seek additional permission from an older child to use data from their younger selves when it is eventually published? At an older age they have a greater capacity for understanding the issues around consent, privacy, and confidentiality.

Now that we have discussed some issues that arose in terms of qualitative research methods, we will examine some interesting findings that emerged from the data.

Musical Childhoods: Global Issues and Local Variations

Global Issues: Digital Technologies and Popular Culture in Children's Lives

In retrospect, the team members had a preliminary hunch not only that we would encounter a substantial amount of music making in homes that has typically been absent in the music education literature but also that we would support the notion that digital technologies would enable many of these experiences. One of the significant shifts in the nature of contemporary childhood that has taken place in recent years, at least in some developed countries, is that children are increasingly confined to the home. Parents then feel responsible to provide activities that can fruitfully occupy children in the home. New technologies enable a wide range of home-based play activities, many of them incorporating music in some form. We assumed, therefore, that technological devices would be a constant in children's lives, in Europe, Asia, Africa, and America, as middle-class commodities. In addition, we speculated that children in different countries would be engaged, to some extent, with different forms of children's popular music and culture, including Disney films and tunes from the top-100 charts. Furthermore, because music features differently in educational curricula across the globe, we expected that there would be some variation in children's school music education experiences.

Some of our initial suspicions were confirmed. Children from all twelve countries engaged with music in the home and there was much variation in terms of their experiences with school music education. However, the use of technological devices was more prominent in some countries than in others, even though all the children came from middle-class households, as locally articulated. This is consistent with discussions on contemporary musical childhoods (see Young, 2009), which suggest differences in terms of access to digital technologies across the globe. But given that our participants were recruited through purposive sampling—individual researchers were invited to recruit children from a cultural and social background similar to their own—it is possible that differences in children's engagement with digital technologies were consistent with and mirrored those of their interviewers. Once again, the issue of researcher situatedness emerges.

Conversely, it was interesting to see how children's popular music and culture existed, to some extent, in the lives of all interviewed children. Disney movies and songs, in particular, were prevalent in most (if not all) homes, following a trend that has been discussed in the past decade or so (Bell, Haas, and Sells, 1995; Bickford, 2011; Campbell, 1998). The same could be said about pop tunes. With the exception of the Kenyan household (where parents were present during the interview with the child), in all other homes, pop music appeared to be a staple in children's lives. Furthermore, in most cases, school music education appeared to play a very small part in children's musical lives. Few child interviewees spoke enthusiastically about their school music experiences. These findings align with the notion that there appears to be a mismatch between musical preferences of seven-year-olds and the repertoires that are typically described in school music curricula. While this is far from a novel issue (see Palheiros and Hargreaves, 2001; Campbell, 1998), it is clear that music education curricula continue to resist some important social changes. As Young (2015) has discussed elsewhere, music education curricula often center on the image of our own pasts, and not the present and the futures of children.

Some also argue that the commercialization of childhood is destabilizing, that it is changing the nature of childhood, even, as some alarmists would claim, "destroying" it (Postman, 1994). Whereas children may have had more limited choices for musical participation in predigital/pre-children's popular music days, they now have to navigate more options. Whether the parents navigate on their children's behalf, whether they allow the children freedom to make their own choices, or whether they compromise by trying to nudge the children into making certain choices rather than directly intervening was an interesting discovery emerging from our observations of parents and the interviews. Parenting styles differ based on different values and ideologies. Gaining insight into the myriad ways that parents structure their children's home musical lives was one aspect of the study we had not entirely anticipated, but this emerged as a point of interest. Musical parenting is a term adopted for babies and very young children, but the concept might be (and we believe should be) extended into older childhood.

However, we should not overplay the significance of new technologies and popular music items in the musical lives of "our" children. There were still plenty of "old" technology musical resources in the form of toys they possessed that provided opportunities for musical play, as well as music-making resources that the children had access to, sometimes items that were not necessarily entirely in their possession. In Israel we saw how Sissi played with a set of musical instruments that belonged to her parents. One interesting aspect we discovered about children at this age was their easy incorporation of all kinds of items in the home into various forms of musical activity and the range and ease with which children achieved this.

We should also acknowledge the extent of conventional musical instruments to which the children had access. Homes had pianos, electronic keyboards, stringed and wind instruments, and percussion instruments. Of course the children in the project were from middle-class homes where there is sufficient income for the purchase of instruments. As the friends and family of music education researchers, participating families were also very likely to be associated in some way with music, education, or the arts, and to value musical pursuits for their children. Some children played these instruments within the structures of formal music instruction, some imitated role models provided by other members of their families, some improvised and made up their own music, and others combined these various ways of playing.

Local Issues: Culture, Individual Differences, and Conceptions of Childhood

As noted in the first chapter, our study initially set out to describe seven-year-olds' musicking (Small, 1998) in the home. Unlike many cross-cultural studies that compare and contrast, our study centered on "describing first" and then juxtaposing information (Rogoff, 2003), focusing predominantly on similarities between children. Regardless of whether these were perceived in some or all seventeen homes with seven-year-olds, we aimed to bring out the experiences and beliefs that were shared. Yet our report would be rendered incomplete and inaccurate if we ignored what was unique about the child participants and their families. Clearly, we cannot give an exhaustive account of all the unique details, but we highlight some of the more striking elements.

An immediate difference was noted regarding variations in the types of homes and how much space was available for musicking. Some children had plenty of access to outdoor spaces and gardens, while others did not. Annie in

Taiwan lived in a comfortable apartment complex. By contrast, Brad and Giovanna lived in spacious homes in the United States and Brazil, respectively. Yet, Giovanna's home was in a secluded and gated community. The spread of such communities has attracted middle-class families (particularly upper-middle class) who can afford this rather expensive lifestyle so to escape the problems of urban violence that are common to everyday life in major Brazilian cities. For those living in gated communities in Brazil, the home is often viewed as a metaphor for a safe space; one that is distanced from urban problems, as well as an "ideal" space for children to grow. The physical characteristics of children's homes certainly played a role in the ways in which they engaged with music in their daily lives.

Culture, religious beliefs, ethnicity, and national identities also impinged on children's lives, including their musical lives. Michael in Kenya was growing up Pentecostal, and Christian tunes were part of his life. Melina in Greece was raised in the Greek Orthodox Christian tradition and showed a preference for Byzantine chants. Sissi in Israel was being raised in the Jewish tradition. At age seven, she had already internalized notions of "us" and "them" (Tajfel, 1978). She knew, for example, that there are at least two ways to keep track of time. Her knowledge of the Jewish (in her own words, "the real") and the Gregorian ("the foreign") calendars was one example of how she negotiated meanings in two cultures, much in the same way that she negotiated musical meanings when engaging with different repertoires.

On that note, the extent to which children were engaged with different types of repertoires constituted another emergent difference. Western "art" music, for example, did not emerge in the discourses of Brazilian children and their families, but had a strong presence in the lives of child participants in the United States, Israel, Singapore, and Taiwan. Likewise, children's music and traditional repertoires (e.g., *maracatu* in Brazil; Byzantine Greek chants) were present in some but not all households. Furthermore, musical practices that could be associated with premature sexualization of childhood emerged in the voices of one Brazilian girl and a Dutch boy, in spite of parental concerns and even relative censorship. Given that these repertoires are far from neutral, but are rather ideologically saturated, the fact that they integrated individual musical childhoods speaks directly to conceptions of children and childhood that were locally adopted.

In addition, the ways in which two (or three) middle-class children from the same country and culture engaged with music in the home revealed many differences. As Tudge (2008) has convincingly argued, there are many differences within cultural groups that are often ignored. Even if our project had more than one child in only four countries (i.e., Brazil, Italy, the Netherlands, and the United States), differences in musical values and practices were evident. These need to be further explored in future research.

Epilogue: Troubling the Global Child in Music Education Research and Practice

The windows on children's musical experiences we gathered in this project offer some insights into the ways in which children learn to see themselves as musical, to know their position in the world in relation to others and to feel a sense of belonging, to a certain social class, ethnicity, and gender. Music as a marker of identity, a social and cultural place-maker, has been written about by many (see Hargreaves, MacDonald, and Miell, 2002). The home, being secluded from the world of peers may allow for more personal and family-oriented forms of musical "identity work." Charlie in the UK was happy to present her musical soft toy and explain how it had been important to her since early childhood, perhaps something she would have been reluctant to do with peers or other adults present. Giovanna in Brazil was proud to show her CDs and recordings of *sertanejo* music along with photos of herself riding a horse. Thus children, as indeed we all do, deliberately shape their musical activities to present themselves in a certain light to whoever is present. The degrees to which the children presented musical activities that conformed to their parents' expectations of a musical childhood, varied across the different countries. Equally, several of the children in "our" project appeared to be manipulating the songs they chose to sing, mindful of who was listening and the connotations those songs carried. At the age of seven many of the children are just beginning to experience the tension between belonging to the musical worlds fashioned by their parents or those of their peers and the commercial worlds of music. Commercial music is supposedly fashioned to cater to children's tastes and needs, but in reality it is designed to create desires that will draw in children for purchase and profit.

As they start to emerge from early childhood into the years of middle childhood, children seek the reassurance of belonging to peer groups and music can act as a marker of belonging. Sometimes the very markers that carry peer group prestige conflict with parental values. Indeed, this conflict is almost axiomatic as children explore ways of being in the world and parents learn to adapt to new changes in family life and parenting. However, interestingly, most of the music activities we collected in this project were solitary and individual. Contemporary families, at least in the families we visited, consist of small numbers of children. While their parents work, children may spend periods of time alone, engaged in solitary activity. There is very little, almost none, of the collective and sociable music activity that might characterize musical experiences beyond the home—at school and in the community. And the sociable musical activity that does take place involves only family members, usually parents, and, interestingly, often the father or maybe an older sibling. As we have highlighted elsewhere, one of the important contributions of the chapters in this are the insights they offer into home-based, solitary music making in contrast to the much more extensive documentation of children's sociable out-of-home musical activities. Moreover, such is the "risk" culture around children that parents tend to confine their children to the home. Compared with former generations, today's children are less free to go out and play with children in the streets and open spaces in their locality (see Malone, 2007). Yet, at the same time, children get "out" into the virtual worlds afforded by the internet and technology, and the outer world reaches deep into the home. Technology considerably widens the scope of music and musical experiences available to children in the home and connects them directly with the wider media and commercial worlds of music, and bypassing their parents. There is, then, an interplay between children's identities and the wider socioeconomic and cultural landscape. We identified this interplay, although also saw that "our" seven-year-olds negotiated this world, often quite deftly, along with the many other forms of musical childhood that emerged in the contexts of school, peers, and family.

But what does this mean for research and practice in music education? Historically speaking, the study of music in children's lives has been dominated by theories and methods derived from developmental psychology. Over the past few decades, a substantial body of knowledge has been constructed around notions of the "universal child." Based on the idea that children develop musically in stages, models and theories of musical development have been formulated, tested, and applied in music education practice. From these works and applications, we have somewhat assumed musical childhood to be a monolith. That is, the notion that children develop musically in a universal manner suggests that they all undergo similar musical experiences as they develop and grow, and, implies, moreover, that the music that is part of their childhood follows, strictly, the characteristics of the Western, tonal system.

While it is probably true that the development of schemata follows specific patterns of maturation, there are some caveats to this logic. First, it is clear that most of what is known about musical development, as is the case with much psychological research, stems from research conducted in North America and Western Europe (Stevens, 2012), or what Heinrich, Heine, and Norenzayan (2010) have called WEIRD societies (i.e., white, educated, industrialized, rich, and democratic). Little is currently known about other societies. Second, the perception of children as musical-meaning makers is fairly recent in the music education literature (see Campbell and Wiggins, 2014). Until fairly recently, the dominant perception of children is that they undergo a "process of becoming" (Young and Ilari, 2012). Third, the ways in which music is presented to children during infancy and childhood and what specific musical behaviors mean (e.g., singing in tune and with a beautiful voice versus the ability to improvise when playing a drum, [see Ilari, 2007, 2013b]) is culture-specific. And finally, the ways in which societies conceive of or define children's musicality and what is expected from them—musically and extramusically—are also social, cultural, and political matters. That is, conceptions of children and childhood are far from universal but are, rather, situated in time, space, political systems, and culture, to name a few.

Our project reinforced what many of us already knew (Young, 2012a), that we should conceptualize musical childhood not as a monolith, but as a plural concept. There are many musical childhoods—as many as there are children in the world. This is evidenced by the fact that even children who grow up in the same family experience the music that is presented to them in a very specific way. As Tudge (2008) has argued, there are many variations within cultures, and we would add, within the family unit. Thus, musical childhoods are not only formed by children's musical proclivities and formal and informal learning experiences, but also shaped by affordances in the home and elsewhere, as well as family values and practices, which, in turn, are nested in the surrounding community and culture. Music education research urgently needs to embrace these ideas.

Note

1. MySpace is a social networking service that is owned by Specific Media LLC and Justin Timberlake. It was founded by Chris DeWolfe and Tom Anderson, and launched in July 2003.

References

Abeles, H. F., and Porter, S. Y. (1978). The sex-stereotyping of musical instruments. *Journal of Research in Music Education, 26*(2), 65–75.

Adachi, M. (2008). Nurturing infants through music at home. Research Grant proposal. Ministry of Education, Culture, Sports, Science and Technology, Japan.

Addessi, A. E. (2009). The musical dimension of the daily routines with under-four children: Changing the diaper, before sleeping, the lunch, free-play. In A. Daubney, E. Longhi, and A. Lamont (Eds.), *Second European conference on developmental psychology of music* (pp. 74–79). London: Roehampton University.

Alldred, P., and Burman, E. (2005). Analysing children's accounts using discourse analysis. In S. Greene and D. Hogan (Eds.), *Researching children's experience: Approaches and methods* (pp. 175–198). London: Sage.

Alwin, D. F. (2003). Parenting practices. In J. Treas and M. Richards (Eds.). *The Blackwell companion to the sociology of families.* Retrieved from http://www.blackwellreference.com.libproxy2.usc.edu/subscriber/uid=1133/tocnode?id=g9780631221586_chunk_g978063122158611

Atterbury, B. W., and Silcox, L. (1993). A comparison of home musical environment and musical aptitude in kindergarten students. *Update: Applications of Research in Music Education, 11*(18), 18–22.

Banks, P. (2011). Cultural socialization in black middle class families. *Cultural Sociology, 61*(1), 61–73. doi: 10.1177/1749975511427646

Barrett, M. (2005). Musical communication and children's communities of musical practice. In D. Miell, R. Macdonald, and D.J. Hargreaves (Eds.), *Musical communication* (pp. 117–142). Oxford: Oxford University Press.

Barrett, M. S. (2011). *A cultural psychology of music education*. New York: Oxford University Press.

Bates, V. (2011). Sustainable music education for poor, white, rural students. *Action, Criticism and Theory for Music Education, 10*(2). Retrieved from http://act.maydaygroup.org/articles/Bates10_2.pdf

Bates, V. (2012). Social class and school music. *Music Educators Journal, 98*(4), 33–37.

Baytiyeh, H., and Pfaffman, J. (2009). Why be a Wikipedian? In C. O'Malley, D. Suthers, P. Reimann, and A. Dimitracopoulou (Eds.), *Proceedings of the ninth international conference on computer supported collaborative learning, vol. 2* (pp. 434–443). Rhodes, Greece: International Society of the Learning Sciences.

Bean, L., and Hott, D. (2005). Wiki: A speedy new tool to manage projects. *Journal of Corporate Accounting and Finance, 16*(5), 3–8.

Bell, E., Haas, L., and Sells, L. (1995). *From mouse to mermaid: The politics of film, gender and culture.* Bloomington: Indiana University Press.

Berger, A. A., and Cooper, S. (2003). Musical play: A case study of preschool children and parents. *Journal of Research in Music Education, 51*(2), 151–165.

Bickford, T. (2011). *Children's music, MP3 players, and expressive practices at a Vermont elementary school: Media consumption as social organization among schoolchildren* (Doctoral dissertation). Retrieved from ProQuest, UMI Dissertations Publishing. (3460625).

Bickford, T. (2012). The new "tween" music industry: The Disney Channel, Kidz Bop and an emerging childhood counterpublic. *Popular Music, 31*, 417–436. doi:10.1017/S0261143012000335

Bidjerano, T., and Newman, J. (2010). Autonomy in after-school choice among preadolescents from Taiwan and the United States. *Journal of Early Adolescence, 30*(5), 733–764.

Bjørkvold, J. R. (1989/1992). *The muse within: Creativity and communication, song and play from childhood through maturity* (W. H. Halverson, Trans.). New York: HarperCollins.

Blacking, J. (1973). *How musical is man?* Seattle: University of Washington Press.

Blacking, J. (1995). *Venda children's songs: A study in ethnomusicological analysis.* Chicago: University of Chicago Press.

Bolam, R., McMahon, S., Stoll, L., Thomas, S., Wallace, M., and Greenwood, A. (2005). *Creating and sustaining effective professional learning communities.* Nottingham, UK: DfES.

Boocock, S. S., and Scott, K. A. (2005). *Kids in context: The sociological study of children and childhoods.* Lanham, MD: Rowman and Littlefield.

Bourdieu, P. (1984). *Distinction: A social critique of the judgment of taste.* Cambridge, MA: Harvard University Press.

Boynton, S., and Kok, R. (Eds.). (2006). *Musical childhoods and the cultures of youth.* Middletown, CT: Wesleyan University Press.

Bradley, R. H., Corwyn, R. F., Pipes McAdoo, H., and García Coll, C. (2001). The home environments of children in the United States. Part I: Variations by age, ethnicity, and poverty status. *Child Development, 72*(6), 1844–1867.

Brittin, R. V. (2000). Children's preference for sequenced accompaniments: The influence of style and perceived tempo. *Journal of Research in Music Education, 48*(3), 237–248.

Bronfenbrenner, U. (1979). *The ecology of human development: Experiments by nature and design.* Cambridge, MA: Harvard University Press.

Brunger, P. (1984). Geschmack für Belcanto- und Pop- Stimmen: Eine repräsentative Untersuchung unter Jugendlichen in einer norddeutschen Großstadt. (Dissertation). University of Hannover.

Buckingham, D. (2011). *The material child: Growing up in consumer culture.* Cambridge, UK: Polity Press.

Burman, E. (1994). *Deconstructing developmental psychology.* London: Routledge.

Byerly, I. (1998). Mirror, mediator and prophet: The music indaba of late-apartheid South Africa. *Ethnomusicology, 42*(1), 1–44.

Campbell, P. S. (1998). *Songs in their heads: Music and its meaning in children's lives.* Oxford: Oxford University Press.

Campbell, P. S. (2002). Ethnomusicology and music education: Crossroads for knowing music, education, and culture. *Research Studies in Music Education, 21*(1), 16–30.

Campbell, P. S. (2006). Global practices. In G. E. McPherson (Ed.), *The child as musician: A handbook of musical development* (pp. 415–437). New York: Oxford University Press.

Campbell, P. S., and Lum, C. (2007). Live and mediated music meant for children. In K. Smithrim and R. Upitis (Eds.), *Listen to their voices: Research and practice in early childhood music. Research to practice III* (pp. 319–329). Waterloo: Canadian Music Educators' Association.

Campbell, P. S., and Wiggins, T. (Eds.). (2014). *The Oxford handbook of children's musical cultures.* Oxford: Oxford University Press.

Carper, K. D. (2001). The effects of repeated exposure and instructional activities on the least preferred of four culturally diverse musical styles with kindergarten and pre-k children. *Bulletin of the Council for Research in Music Education, 151*, 41–50.

Cassidy, C., Christie, D., Coutts, N., Dunn, J., Sinclair, C., Skinner, D., and Wilson, A. (2008). Building communities of educational enquiry. *Oxford Review of Education, 34*(2), 217–235.

Castaños, C., and Piercy, P. F. (2010). The wiki as a virtual space for qualitative data collection. *Qualitative Report, 15*(4), 948–955.

Childhood Studies. *Oxford bibliographies.* Retrieved from https://global.oup.com/academic/product/oxford-bibliographies-in-childhood-studies-9780199791231?cc=us&lang=en&

Clarke, E., Dibben, N., and Pitts, S. (2008). *Music and mind in everyday life.* Oxford: Oxford University Press.

Cohen, V. W. (1980). *The emergence of musical gestures in kindergarten children.* (Unpublished doctoral dissertation). University of Illinois.

Colley, A. (2008). Young people's musical taste: Relationship with gender and gender related traits. *Journal of Applied Social Psychology, 38*(8), 2039–2055.

Colley, A., Mulhern, G., Relton, S., and Shafi, S. (2008). Exploring children's stereotypes through drawings: The case of musical performance. *Social Development, 18*(2), 464–477.

Comber, C., Hargreaves, D. J., and Colley, A. (1993). Girls, boys, and technology in music education. *British Journal of Music Education*, 10, 123–134.

Confucius. (2001). *The analects* (A. Waley, Trans.). New York: Knopf. (Original translation published 1938).

Cook, D. T., and Kaiser, S. B. (2004). Betwixt and between: Age ambiguity and the sexualization of the female consuming subject. *Journal of Consumer Culture 4*(2), 203–227. doi: 10.1177/1469540504043682

Corsaro, W. A. (2003). *We're friends right? Inside kid's culture.* Washington, DC: Joseph Henry Press.

Corsaro, W. A. (2011). *The sociology of childhood. Third Edition.* Thousand Oaks, CA: Pine Forge Press.

Corsaro, W. A., and Eder, D. (1990). Children's peer cultures. *Annual Review of Sociology*, 16, 197–220.

Corsaro, W. A., and Molinari, L. (2001). Entering and observing in children's worlds: A reflection on a longitudinal ethnography of early education in Italy. In P. Christensen and A. James (Eds.), *Research with children: Perspectives and practices* (pp. 179–200). London: Routledge/Falmer.

Creech, A. (2009). Teacher-pupil-parent triads: A typology of interpersonal interaction in the context of learning a musical instrument. *Musicae Scientiae, 13*(2), 387–413.
Creech, A., and Hallam. S. (2003). Parent-teacher-pupil interactions in instrumental music tuition: A literature review. *British Journal of Music Education, 20*, 29–44.
Creswell, J. (2011). *Educational research: Planning, conducting, and evaluating quantitative and qualitative research.* Upper Saddle River, NJ: Pearson.
Custodero, L. (2006). Singing practices in 10 families with young children. *Journal of Research in Music Education, 54*(1), 37–56.
Custodero, L., and Johnson-Green, E. (2003). Passing the cultural torch: Musical experience and musical parenting of infants. *Journal of Research in Music Education, 51*(2), 102–114.
Davidson, J. W., Howe, M. J. A., Moore, D. G., and Sloboda, J. A. (1996). The role of parental influences in the development of musical performance. *British Journal of Developmental Psychology, 14*, 399–412.
Dean, B. (2015). A hidden world of song: Exploring the everyday singing lives of three and four year old children at home. Paper presented at the Twentieth National Conference of the Australian Society for Music Education. Retrieved from http://asme2015.com.au/
De Grätzer, D. P. (1999). Can music help to improve parent-child communication? *International Journal of Music Education, 34*(1), 47–56.
Delalande, F. (2009). *La nascita della musica.* Milan: FrancoAngeli.
Deleuze, G., and Guattari, F. (1987). *A thousand plateaus: Capitalism and schizophrenia.* Minneapolis: University of Minnesota Press.
DeNora, T. (2000). *Music in everyday life.* Cambridge: Cambridge University Press.
DeVries, P. (2009). Music at home with the under fives: What is happening? *Early Child Development and Care, 179*(4), 395–405.
Dibben, N. (2002). Gender, identity and music. In R. Macdonald, D. Hargreaves, and D. Miell (Eds.), *Musical identities* (pp. 117–133). New York: Oxford University Press.
Eijkman, H. (2010). Academics and Wikipedia: Reframing Web 2.0+as a disruptor of traditional academic power-knowledge arrangements. *Campus-Wide Information Systems, 27*(3), 173–185.
Eisner, E. (2002). *The arts and the creation of mind.* New Haven, CT: Yale University Press.
Epstein, J. L. (2001). *School, family, and community partnerships: Preparing educators and improving schools.* Boulder, CO: Westview Press.
Fleer, M., Hedegaard, M., and Tudge, J. R. H. (2008). Constructing childhood: Global-local policies and practices. In M. Fleer, M. Hedegaard, and J. R. H. Tudge (Eds.), *Childhood studies and the impact of globalization: Policies and practices at global and local levels* (pp. 1–20). New York: Routledge.
Flohr, J., and Persellin, D. (2011). Applying brain research to children's musical experiences. In S. Burton and C. Taggart (Eds.), *Learning from young children: Research in early childhood music* (pp. 3–22). Lanham, MD: Rowman and Littlefield.
Folkestad, G. (2006). Formal and informal learning situations or practices vs formal and informal ways of learning. *British Journal of Music Education, 23*(2), 135–145.
Fung, C., and Gromko, J. (2001). Effects of active versus passive listening on the quality of children's invented notations and preferences for two pieces from an unfamiliar culture. *Psychology of Music, 29*(2), 128–138.

Furedi, F. (2001). *Paranoid parenting: Why ignoring the experts may be best for your child.* Chicago: Chicago Review Press.

García Coll, C., Akiba, D., Palacios, N., Bailey, B., Silver, R., DiMartino, L., and Chin, C. (2002). Parental involvement in children's education: Lessons from three immigrant groups. *Parenting, 2*(3), 303–324.

García Coll, C., and Marks, A. K. (2009). *Immigrant stories: Ethnicity and academics in middle-childhood.* Oxford: Oxford University Press.

Gaunt, H. (2005). Instrumental/vocal teaching and learning in conservatoires: A case study of teachers' perceptions. In G. Odam and N. Bannan (Eds.), *The reflective conservatoire* (pp. 245–267). Abingdon: Ashgate.

Gears, D. A. (2011). *Wiki behavior in the workplace: Emotional aspects of content development.* (Doctoral dissertation). Available through ProQuest Dissertations and Theses database. (AAT 3473274).

Geertz, C. (1973). *The interpretation of cultures.* New York: Basic Books.

Gembris, H., and Schellberg, G. (2003). *Music in primary schools*: Ofsted Subject Reports Series 2001/2. London: OFSTED.

Gibson, P., Norris, E., and Alcock, P. (1992). *Music: The rock classic connection.* Oxford: Oxford University Press.

Giles, J. (2005). Internet encyclopedias go head to head. *Nature, 438*, 900–901.

Giliomee, H., and Mbenga, B. (2007). *New history of South Africa.* Cape Town: Tafelberg.

Gillen, J., and Cameron, A. (Eds.). (2010). *International perspectives on early childhood research: A day in the life.* London: Palgrave Macmillan.

Gluschankof, C. (2009). Preschool children performing their own musical compositions: A glimpse to creative processes. In J. Xie (Ed.), *Proceedings of the 2009 National Music Education Conference of China, China Conservatory, Beijing, China, 23–25 August 2009* (pp. 104–113). Beijing: CSME and China Conservatory.

Gluschankof, C. I. (2005). *Spontaneous musical behaviors in Israeli Jewish and Arab kindergartens: Searching for universal principles within cultural differences.* (Unpublished doctoral dissertation). Hebrew University of Jerusalem.

Goodnow, J., and Collins, W. A. (1990). *Development according to parents: The nature, sources and consequences of parents' ideas.* Hillsdale, NJ: Erlbaum.

Green, L. (1997). *Music, gender, education.* Cambridge: Cambridge University Press.

Green, L. (2002). Exposing the gendered discourse of music education. *Feminism and Psychology, 12*(2), 137–144.

Greer, R. D., Dorow, L. G., and Randall, A. (1974). Music listening preferences of elementary school children. *Journal of Research in Music Education, 22*, 284–291.

Gregory, K., and Clarke, M. (2003). High-stakes assessment in England and Singapore. *Theory into Practice, 42*(1), 56–74.

Griffin, S. M. (2011). Through the eyes of children: Telling insights into music experiences. *Visions of Research in Music Education, 18*. Retrieved from http://www-usr.rider.edu/vrme~/

Hall, C. (2005). Gender and boys' singing in early childhood. *British Journal of Music Education, 22*(1), 5–20.

Hargreaves, D. J. (1982). The development of aesthetic reaction to music. *Psychology of Music*, Special Issue, 51–54.

Hargreaves, D. J. (1987). *The developmental psychology of music*. Cambridge: Cambridge University Press.

Hargreaves, D. J., Macdonald, R., and Miell, D. (Eds.). (2002). Musical identities. Oxford: Oxford University Press.

Hargreaves, D. J., and North, A. (Eds.). (1998). *The social psychology of music*. Oxford: Oxford University Press.

Hargreaves, D. J., North, A. C., and Tarrant, M. (2006). Musical preference and taste in childhood and adolescence. In G. McPherson (Ed.), *The child as musician* (pp. 135–154). New York: Oxford University Press.

Harrison, A. C., and O'Neill, S. A. (2000). Children's gender-typed preferences for musical instruments: An intervention study. *Psychology of Music, 28*, 81–97.

Hedegaard, M. (2012). Children's creative modeling of conflict resolution as central in their learning and development in families. In M. Hedegaard, K. Aronsson, A. Højholt, and O. S. Ulvik (Ed.), *Children, childhood and everyday life* (pp. 55–74). Charlotte, NC: Information Age.

Hedegaard, M., Aronsson, K., Højholt, A., and Ulvik, O. S. (Eds.). (2012). *Children, childhood, and everyday life*. Charlotte, NC: Information Age.

Heinrich, J., Heine, S. J., and Norenzayan, A. (2010). The weirdest people in the world? Working Paper Series des Rates für Sozial- und Wirtschaftsdaten, No. 139. Available at http://hdl.handle.net/10419/43616

Heunis, L. (Ed.). (1993). *Musical learning and learning musically*. Bloemfontein, South Africa: University of the Orange Free State.

Himonides, E. (2012). The misunderstanding of music technology education: A meta perspective. In G. McPherson and G. Welch (Eds.), *Oxford handbook of music education*, vol. 2 (pp. 433–455). Oxford: Oxford University Press.

Hollingshead, A. A. (1975). *Four-factor index of social status*. Unpublished manuscript, Yale University, New Haven, CT.

Howard, J. R. (1992). Contemporary Christian music: Where rock meets religion. *Journal of Popular Culture, 26*(1), 123–130.

Howe, M. J. A., and Sloboda, J. (1991). Young musicians' accounts of significant influences in their early lives. 1. The family and the musical background. *British Journal of Music Education, 8*, 39–52.

Huang, C., and Lamb, M. (2015). Are Chinese children more compliant? Examination of the cultural difference in observed maternal control and child compliance. *Journal of Cross-Cultural Psychology, 46*(1), 150–167.

Huang, H. (2012). Why Chinese people play Western classical music: Transcultural roots of music philosophy. *International Journal of Music Education, 30*, 161–176.

Hviid, P. (2012). "Remaining the same" and children's experience of development. In M. Hedegaard, K. Aronsson, C. Hojholt and O. S. Ulvik (Eds.), *Children, childhood, and everyday life: Children's perspectives* (pp. 37–52). Charlotte, NC: Information Age.

Ilari, B. (2005). On musical parenting of young children: Musical beliefs and behaviors of mothers and infants. *Early Child Development and Care, 175* (7 and 8), 647–660. doi:10.1080/0300443042000302573

Ilari, B. (2007). Musical development of Brazilian children: Regionalisms, style and identity. In D. Pistone and Z. Chueke (Eds.), *Brésil Musical: Cahiers du Colloque* (pp. 65–81). Paris: Zurfluh.

Ilari, B. (2009). Por uma conduta ética na pesquisa musical envolvendo seres humanos. In R.Budasz (Ed.), *Pesquisa em música no Brasil: métodos, domínios e perspectivas* (pp. 167–198). Available from http://www.anppom.com.br/editora/Pesquisa_em_Musica-01.pdf

Ilari, B. (2011). Twenty-first-century parenting, electronic media and early childhood music education. In S. L. Burton and C. C. Taggart (Eds.), *Learning from young children: Research in early childhood music* (pp. 195–213). Lanham, MD: Rowman and Littlefield.

Ilari, B. (2013). Concerted cultivation and music learning: Global issues and local variations. *Research Studies in Music Education*, 35(2), 179–196. doi: 10.1177/1321103X13509348

Ilari, B. (2014). Musical cultures of girls in the Brazilian Amazon. In P. S. Campbell and T. Wiggins (Eds.), *Oxford handbook of children's musical cultures* (pp. 131–146). Oxford: Oxford University Press.

Ilari, B., and Chitwood, A. (2016, March). Singing practices in monolingual and bilingual families with toddlers. In B. Ilari (Chair), Music Learning in Childhood and Family Dynamics. Symposium conducted at the meeting of the National Association for Music Education, Atlanta, GA.

Ilari, B., Moura, A., and Bourscheidt, L. (2011). Between interactions and commodities: Musical parenting of infants and toddlers in Brazil. *Music Education Research*, 13(1), 51–67. doi: 10.1080/14613808.2011.553277

Ito, M., Horst, H. A., Matteo Bittanti, M., Boyd, D., Stephenson, B. H., Lange, P. G., Pascoe, C. J., and Robinson, L. (2009). *Living and learning with new media: Summary of findings from the Digital Youth Project in the John D. and Catherine T. MacArthur Foundation Reports on Digital Media and Learning.* Cambridge, MA: MIT Press.

James, A. (2011). Agency. In J. Qvortrup, W. A. Corsaro, and M. S. Honig (Eds.), *The Palgrave handbook of childhood studies* (pp. 34–45), New York: Palgrave Macmillan.

James, A., Jenks, C., and Prout, A. (1998). *Theorizing childhood.* Cambridge, UK: Blackwell.

James, A., and Prout, A. (1997). *Constructing and reconstructing childhood: Contemporary issues in the sociological study of childhood* (2nd ed.). London: Routledge.

Jellison, J. A., and Flowers, P. J. (1991). Talking about music: Interviews with disabled and nondisabled children. *Journal of Research in Music Education, 39*(3), 322–333.

Jenkins, H. (2006). *Convergence culture: Where old and new media collide.* New York: New York University Press.

Jenks, C. (1996). *Childhood*. London: Routledge.

Johnson-Green, E. A., and Custodero, L. A. (2002). Toddler top 40: Musical preference of babies, toddlers, and their parents. *Journal of Zero-to-Three*, 23(1), 47–48.

Kanellopoulos, P. A. (2010). Towards a sociological perspective on researching children's creative music making practices: An exercise in self-consciousness. In R. Wright (Ed.), *Sociology and Music Education* (pp. 115–138). Farnham, UK: Ashgate.

Kaplan, A. M., and Haenlein, M. (2010). Users of the world, unite! The challenges and opportunities of Social Media. *Business Horizons* 53(1), 59–68.

Kaufman, P. (2005). Middle-class social reproduction: The activation and negotiation of structural advantage. *Sociological Forum, 20*(2), 245–270.

Kehily, M. J. (2008). *An introduction to childhood studies* (2nd ed.). Oxford: Oxford University Press.

Kelley, L., and Sutton-Smith, B. (1987). A study of infant musical productivity. In J. C. Peery, I. W. Peery, and T. W. Drapers (Eds.), *Music and child development* (pp. 35–53). New York: Springer.

Kerchner, J., and Abril, C. (2009). (Eds.). *Music in our lives: Experiences we have and meanings we make.* Lanham, MD: Rowman and Littlefield.

Kim, H. J., Miller, H. R., Herbert, B., Pedersen, S., and Loving, C. (2012). Using a wiki in a scientist-teacher professional learning community: Impact on teacher perception changes. *Journal of Science Education and Technology, 21*(4), 440–452.

Kinney, A. B. (Ed.). (1995). *Chinese views of childhood.* Honolulu: University of Hawaii Press.

Kohn, M. L. (1963). Social class and parent-child relationships: An interpretation. *American Journal of Sociology, 68*(4), 471–480.

Kohn, M. L. (1995). Social structure and personality through time and space. In P. Moen, G. H. Elder Jr., and K. Lüscher (Eds.), *Examining lives in context: Perspectives on the ecology of human development* (pp. 141–168). Washington, DC: American Psychological Association.

Kok, R.-M. (2006). Music for a postcolonial child: Theorizing Malaysian memories. In S. Boynton, and R.-M. Kok (Eds.), *Musical childhoods and the cultures of youth* (pp. 89–104). Middletown, CT: Wesleyan University Press, 2006.

Kolbitsch, J., and Maurer, H. (2006). The transformation of the web: How emerging communities shape the information we consume. *Journal of Universal Computer Science, 12*(2), 187–213.

Kopiez, R., and Lehmann, M. (2008). The "open-earedness" hypothesis and the development of age-related aesthetic reactions to music in elementary school children. *British Journal of Music Education, 25*(2), 121–138.

Koutsoupidou, T. (2008). Effects of different teaching styles on the development of musical creativity: Insights from interviews with music specialists. *Musicae Scientiae, 12*(2), 311–335.

Koutsoupidou, T., and Hargreaves, D. J. (2009). An experimental study of the effects of improvisation on the development of creative thinking in music. *Psychology of Music, 37*(3), 251–278.

Kremer-Sadlik, T., and Fatigante, M. (2015). Investing in children's future: Cross-cultural perspectives and ideologies on parental involvement in education. *Childhood, 22*(1), 67–84.

K'ung-fu Tzu (Confucius). (2008). *The Li Chi or book of rites, part II of II* (J. Legge, Trans.). Tampa, FL: Forgotten Books. (Original work published 1885).

La Gorce, T. (2006, November 26). Market for hipsters-in-training. *New York Times.* Retrieved from http://www.nytimes.com/2006/11/26/arts/music/26lago.html?_r=1&oref=slogin

Lamont, A. (2002). Musical identities and the school environment. In R. Macdonald, D. Hargreaves, and D. Miell (Eds.), *Musical identities* (pp. 41–59). New York: Oxford University Press.

Lamont, A. (2008). Young children's musical worlds: Musical engagement in 3.5-year-olds. *Journal of Early Childhood Research, 6*(3), 247–261.

Lancy, D. (2008). *The anthropology of childhood.* Cambridge: Cambridge University Press.

Lange, A., and Mierendorff, J. (2011). Method and methodology in childhood research. In J. Qvortrup, W. A. Corsaro, and M. S. Honig (Eds.), *The Palgrave handbook of childhood studies* (pp. 78–95). New York: Palgrave Macmillan.

Lareau, A. (2010). Concerted cultivation and the accomplishment of natural growth. In K. Sternheimer (Ed.), *Childhood in American society* (pp. 237–246). Boston: Allyn and Bacon.

Lareau, A. (2011). *Unequal childhoods: Class, race, and family life* (2nd ed.), *with an update a decade later.* Berkeley: University of California Press.

Leadbeater, C. (2008). *We-think: Mass innovation, not mass production: The power of mass creativity.* London: Proile Books.

LeBlanc, A. (1979). Generic style music preferences of fifth-grade students. *Journal of Research in Music Education, 27,* 255–270.

LeBlanc, A. (1981). Effects of style, tempo, and performing medium on children's music preference. *Journal of Research in Music Education, 29*(2), 143–156.

LeBlanc, A. (1991). Effect of maturation/aging on music listening preference: A review of the literature. Paper presented at the Ninth National Symposium on Research in Music Behavior, School of Music, Michigan State University, Cannon Beach, Oregon, March 7–9.

LeBlanc, A., Sims, W., Siivola, C., and Obert, M. (1996). Music style preferences of different age listeners. *Journal of Research in Music Education, 44*(1), 49–59.

Leuf, B., and Cunningham, W. (2001). *The wiki way: Quick collaboration on the web.* Boston: Addison-Wesley.

Loots, A. G. J. (1997). *A critical approach to rock music from a cultural-historical and theoretical perspective.* (Unpublished doctoral dissertation). University of Port Elizabeth, South Africa.

Lucia, C. (1992). Ethnomusicology and the art of the state: Training the music professional in South Africa. In J. Van Tonder (Ed.), *Music matters: Music education in the 1990s* (pp. 75–86). Cape Town: University of Cape Town.

Lum, C. H. (2008). Home musical environment of children in Singapore. *Journal of Research in Music Education, 56*(2), 101–117.

Lum, C. H., and Dairianathan, E. (2013). Reflexive and reflective perspectives of musical childhoods in Singapore. In P. S. Campbell and T. Wiggins (Eds.), *The Oxford handbook of children's musical cultures* (pp. 332–349). New York: Oxford University Press.

Lum, C. H., and Whiteman, P. (Eds.). (2012). *Musical childhoods of Asia and the Pacific.* Charlotte, NC: Information Age.

Mackinlay, E. (2012). Speaking autoethnographically and singing maternally. In C. H. Lum and P. Whiteman (Eds.), *Musical childhoods of Asia and the Pacific* (pp. 37–56). Charlotte, NC: Information Age.

Magubane. P. (1998). *Vanishing cultures of South Africa.* Cape Town: Struik.

Mahoney, J. L., Larson, R. W., Eccles, J. S., and Lord, H. (2005). Organized activities as developmental contexts for children and adolescents. In J. L. Mahoney,

R. W. Larson, and J. S. Eccles (Eds.), *Organized activities as contexts of development* (pp. 3–22). Mahwah, NJ: Lawrence Erlbaum.

Malone, K. (2007). The bubble-wrap generation: Children growing up in walled gardens. *Environmental Education Research, 13*(4), 513–527.

Mandela, N. (1999). Speech to the Parliament of the world's religions. In *Council for the Parliament of the World Religions*. Retrieved April 19, 2013 from http://www.parliamentofreligions.org/index.cfm?n=4andsn=43

Marsh, K. (2009). *The musical playground*. Oxford: Oxford University Press.

Marshall, N., and Shibazaki, K. (2013). The development of gender associated attitudes, preferences and interactions to musical instruments: Sound and image. *Music Education Research, 15*(4), 406–420.

Mathison, S. (1988). Why triangulate? *Educational Researcher, 17*(2), 13–17.

Matsunobu, K., and Bresler, L. (2013). Qualitative research in music education: Concepts, goals and characteristics. In C. Conway (Ed.), *Qualitative research in American music education* (pp. 21–39). Oxford: Oxford University Press.

Mayer, S. E. (2002). *The influence of parental income on children's outcomes*. Wellington, NZ: Knowledge Management Group, Ministry of Social Development, Te Manatu Whakahiato Ora.

Mayfield, A. (2008). What is social media? Retrieved from http://www.icrossing.co.uk/fileadmin/uploads/eBooks/What_is_Social_Media_iCrossing_ebook.pdf

McKoy, C. (2003). A review of research on instructional approach and world music preference. *Update: Applications of Research in Music Education, 22*(1), 36–43.

McPherson, G. (2009). The role of parents in children's musical development. *Psychology of Music, 37*(1), 91–110.

Mehr, S. (2014). Music in the home: New evidence for an intergenerational link. *Journal of Research in Music Education, 62*(1), 78–88.

Millar, B. (2008). Selective hearing: Gender bias in the musical preferences of young adults. *Psychology of Music*, 36(4), 429–445.

Miller, T., and Shahriari, A. (2009).*World music: A global journey* (2nd ed.). New York: Routledge.

Milovanovic, M., Minovic, M., Stavljanin, V., Savkovic, M., and Starcevic, D. (2012). Wiki as a corporate learning tool: Case study for software development company. *Behaviour and Information Technology, 31*(8), 767–777.

Minkenberg, H. (1991). Das Musikerleben von Kindern im Alter von fünf bis zehn Jahren. Frankfurt a. m.: Peter Lang.

Montgomery, A. (1996). Effect of tempo on music preferences of children in elementary and middle school. *Journal of Research in Music Education, 44*(2), 134–146.

Montgomery, H. (2009). *An introduction to childhood: Anthropological perspectives on children's lives*. Oxford: Blackwell.

Moorhead, G. E., Sandvik, F., and Wight, D. (1951/1978). Free use of instruments for musical growth. In *Music of young children* (pp. 91–117). Santa Barbara, CA: Pillsbury Foundation for Advancement of Music Education.

Mualem, O., and Klein, P. (2011). The communicative characteristics of musical interactions compared with play interactions between mothers and their one-year-old infants. *Early Child Development and Care, 183*(7), 899–915.

Navera, G. S. (2013). The Singapore arts landscape: Influences, tensions, confluences, and possibilities for the learning context. In C. H. Lum (Ed.), *Contextualized practices in music education: An international dialogue on Singapore* (pp. 3–20). Dordrecht: Springer.
No! (2012, November 12). Retrieved December 5, 2012, from Wikipedia, http://en.wikipedia.org/wiki/No!
North, A. C., and Hargreaves, D. (2008). *The social and applied psychology of music.* Oxford: Oxford University Press.
North, A. C., Hargreaves, D. J., and O'Neill, S. A. (2000). The importance of music to adolescents. *British Journal of Educational Psychology, 70*, 255–272.
Oerhle, E. (1988). *A new direction for South African music education.* Pietermaritzburg: Shuter and Shooter.
O'Neill, S. A. (1997). Gender and music. In D.J. Hargreaves and A. North (Eds.), *The social psychology of music* (pp. 46–63). Oxford: Oxford University Press.
O'Neill, S. A. (2002). Crossing the divide: Feminist perspectives on gender and music. *Feminism and Psychology, 12*(2), 133–136.
O'Neill, S. A., and Boulton, M. J. (1996). Boys' and girls' preferences for musical instruments: A function of gender? *Psychology of Music, 24*(2), 171–183.
Opie, I., and Opie, P. (1988). *The singing game.* Oxford: Oxford University Press.
Ozturk, I. H. (2012). Wikipedia as a teaching tool for technological pedagogical content knowledge: Development in pre-service history teacher education. *Educational Research and Reviews, 7*(7), 182–191.
Palheiros, G., and Hargreaves, D. J. (2001). Listening to music at home and school. *British Journal of Music Education, 18*(2), 103–118.
Parameswaran, M., and Whinston, A. B. (2007a). Social computing: An overview. *Communications of the Association for Information Systems, 19*, 762–780.
Parameswaran, M., and Whinston, A. B. (2007b). Research issues in social computing. *Journal of the Association for Information Systems, 8*(6), 336–350.
Parncutt, R. (2009). Prenatal development and the phylogeny and ontogeny of musical behaviour. In S. Hallam, I. Cross, and M. Thaut (Eds.), *Oxford handbook of music psychology* (pp. 219–228). Oxford: Oxford University Press.
Pérez, J., and Young, S. (2010). Using a wiki to underpin research: An international project about children's everyday musical activity. Presented at *Literacy Research Centre Seminar Series.* Lancaster University, Lancaster, UK.
Peters, M., Seeds, K., Goldstein, A. and Coleman, N. (2008). *Parental involvement in children's education 2007.* Research Report. Nottingham, UK: DCSF-RR034.
Postman, N. (1994). *The disappearance of childhood.* New York: Random House.
Pugh, A. J. (2009). *Longing and belonging: Parents, children, and consumer culture.* Berkeley: University of California Press.
Ravallion, M. (2010). The developing world's bulging (but vulnerable) middle class. *World Development, 38*(4), 445–454.
Roberts, D., Foehr, U., and Rideout, V. (2005). *Generation M: Media in the lives of 8–18 year-olds.* Menlo Park, CA: Henry J. Kaiser Family Foundation. Retrieved from www.kff.org/entmedia/7251.cfm
Rogoff, B. (2003). *The cultural nature of human development.* Oxford: Oxford University Press.

Rose, N. (1999). *Powers of freedom: Reframing political thought.* Cambridge: Cambridge University Press.

Roulston, K. (2006). Qualitative investigation of young children's music preferences. *International Journal of Education and the Arts, 7*(9). Retrieved from http://ijea.asu.edu/v7n9/

Saldaña, J. (2010). *Fundamentals of qualitative research: Understanding qualitative research.* New York: Oxford University Press.

Sauer, I., Bialek, D., Efimova, E., Schwartlander, R., Pless, G., and Neuhaus, P. (2005). "Blogs" and "Wikis" are valuable software tools for communication within research groups. *Artificial Organs,* 29(1), 82–83.

Schellberg, G. (2006). Development of musical preferences of elementary school children. Paper presented at the 9th International Conference on Music Perception and Cognition (Bologna: Alma Mater Studiorum University of Bologna.

Schellberg, G., and Gembris, H. (2004). Was Grundschulkinder (nicht) hören wollen: Eine neue Studie über Musikpräferenzen von Kindern der 1. bis 4. Klasse. *Musik in der Grundschule,* (4): 48–52.

Schousboue, I. (2005). Local and global perspectives on the everyday lives of children. *Culture and Psychology, 11*(2), 207–225.

Schuckert, R. F., and McDonald, R. L. (1968). An attempt to modify the musical preferences of preschool children. *Journal of Research in Music Education, 16,* 39–44.

Shehan, P. K. (1984). The effect of instruction method on preference, achievement, and attentiveness for Indonesian gamelan music. *Psychology of Music, 12,* 34–42.

Sichivitsa, V. O. (2007). The influences of parents, teachers, peers and other factors on students' motivation in music. *Research Studies in Music Education, 29,* 55–68.

Sims, W., and Cassidy, J. (1997). Verbal and operant responses of young children to vocal versus instrumental song performances. *Journal of Research in Music Education,* 45(2), 234–244.

Sloboda, J. (2001). Emotion, functionality, and the everyday experience of music: Where does music education fit? *Music Education Research,* 3(2), 243–254.

Small, C. (1998). *Musicking: The meanings of performing and listening.* Middletown, CT: Wesleyan University Press.

Social Computing. (n.d.). Retrieved September 15, 2012, from Wikipedia. http://en.wikipedia.org/wiki/Social_computing

Spera, C. (2006). Adolescents' perceptions of parental goals, practices, and styles in relation to their motivation and achievement. *Journal of Early Adolescence,* 26(4), 456–490.

Steinberg, S. R., and Kincheloe, J. L. (Eds.). (1997). *Kinderculture: The corporate construction of childhood.* Boulder, CO: Westview Press.

Stevens, C. (2012). Music perception and cognition: A review of recent cross-cultural research. *Topics in Cognitive Science* (July), 1–15. doi:10.1111/j.1756-8765.2012.01215.x

St. John, P. (2009). Growing up and growing old: Communities in counterpoint. *Early Child Development and Care,* 179(6), 733–746.

Swanwick, K., and Tillman, J. (1986). The sequence of musical development: A study of children's composition. *British Journal of Music Education,* 3(3), 305–340.

Tajfel, H. (1978). *Differentiation between social groups: Studies in the social psychology of intergroup relations.* London: Academic Press.

Takahashi, M. (2013). Young children's character culture in Japan: Possession, knowledge and belongingness. *Childhoods Today*, *7*(1). Retrieved from http://www.childhoodstoday.org/article.php?id=72

Tarrant, M., North, A., and Hargreaves, D. J (2002).Youth identity and music. In R. Macdonald, D. Hargreaves, and D. Miell (Eds.), *Musical identities* (pp. 134–150). New York: Oxford University Press.

Tenenbaum, H. R., and Leaper, C. (2002). Are parents gender schemas related to their children's gender-related cognitions? *Developmental Psychology*, *38*(4), 615–630.

Thompson, L. (2001). *A history of South Africa* (3rd ed.). New Haven, CT: Yale University Press.Triandis, H. (1995). *Individualism and collectivism*. Boulder, CO: Westview Press.

Tudge, J. H. R. (2008). *The everyday lives of young children: Culture, class and child rearing in diverse societies*. Cambridge: Cambridge University Press.

Tudge, J. R. H., Lopes, R. S., Piccinini, C. A., Sperb, T. M., Chipenda-Dansokho, S., Marin, A. H., Vivian, A. G., Oliveira, D. S., Sonego, J., Frizzo, G. B., and Freitas, L. B. L. (2013). Parents' child-rearing values in southern Brazil: Mutual influences of social class and children's development. *Journal of Family Issues*, *34*(10), 1379–1400.

Tudge, J. H. R., Odero, D., Piccinini, C. A., Doucet, F., Sperb, T. M., and Lopes, R. S. (2006). A window into different cultural worlds: Young children's everyday activities in the United States, Brazil, and Kenya. *Child Development*, *77*, 1446–1469.

Turino, T. (2006). *Music as social life: The politics of participation*. Champaign: University of Illinois Press.

Turkle, S. (1995). *Life on the screen: Identity in the age of the internet*. New York: Touchstone.

UN General Assembly. (1948). *Universal Declaration of Human Rights*. Article 26. Retrieved from http://www.un.org/en/documents/udhr/index.shtml#a26

Van Tonder, J. (Ed.). (1992). *Music matters: Music education in the 1990s*. Cape Town: University of Cape Town.

Vincent, C., and Ball, S. J. (2007). Making up the middle-class child: Families, activities and class dispositions. *Sociology*, *41*(6), 1061–1077.

Vygotsky, L. S. (1935/1994). The problem of the environment. In R. Van der Meer and J. Valsiner (Eds.), *The Vygotsky reader* (pp. 338–354). Oxford: Basil Blackwell.

Weisner, T. S. (1996). Why ethnography should be the most important method of study of human development. In R. Jessor, A. Colby, and R. A. Shweder (Eds.), *Ethnography and human development: Context and meaning in social inquiry* (pp. 305–324). Chicago: University of Chicago Press.

Welch, G. F. (2011). Culture and gender in a cathedral music context: An activity theory exploration. In M. S. Barrett (Ed.), *A cultural psychology of music education* (pp. 225–258). New York: Oxford University Press.

Wenger, E. (1999). *Communities of practice*. Cambridge: Cambridge University Press.

Wentzel, K. R. (1998). Parents' aspirations for children's educational attainment: Relations to parental beliefs and social address variables. *Merrill-Palmer Quarterly*, *44*, 20–37.

Westcott, H. L., and Littleton, K. S. (2005). Exploring meaning in interviews with children. In S. Greene and D. Hogan (Eds.), *Researching children's experiences: Approaches and methods* (pp. 145–157). London: Sage.
Wheeler, S., Yeomans, P., and Wheeler, D. (2008). The good, the bad and the wiki: Evaluating student-generated content for collaborative learning, *British Journal of Educational Technology*. 39(6), 987–995.
Whiteman, P. (2014). The complex ecologies of early childhood musical cultures in Australia and Hawaii. In P. S. Campbell and T. Wiggins (Eds.), *The Oxford handbook of children's musical cultures* (pp. 466–478). New York: Oxford University Press.
Whiteman, P., and Lum, C. (Eds.). (2012). *Musical childhoods of Asia and the Pacific*. Charlotte, NC: Information Age.
Williams, K. E., Barrett, M. S., Welch, G. F., Abad, V., and Broughton, M. (2015). Associations between early shared music activities in the home and later child outcomes: Findings from the longitudinal study of Australian children. *Early Childhood Research Quarterly*, *31*, 113–124. doi: 10.1016/j.ecresq.2015.01.004
Wolff, T. E. (2009). The PIUG wiki. Communication and collaboration par excellence. *Searcher: The Magazine for Database professionals*, *17*(8), 12–19 and 51–53.
Woodhead, M. (1999). Reconstructing developmental psychology: Some first steps. *Children and Society*, 13, 3–19.
Woodward, S. C. (1994). The impact of current functions of music in children's lives on music education philosophies. In H. Lees (Ed.), *Musical connections: Tradition and change* (pp. 7–13). London: International Society for Music Education.
Woodward, S. C. (2007). Nation building–one child at a time: Early childhood music education in South Africa. *Arts Education Policy Review*. *109*(2), 33–42.
Wright, R. (2010). (Ed.). *Sociology and music education*. Farnham: Ashgate.
Young, S. (2006). Seen but not heard: Young children, improvised singing and educational practice. *Contemporaries Issues in Early Childhood*, *7*(3), 270–280.
Young, S. (2008). Lullaby light shows: Everyday musical experience among under twos. *International Journal of Music Education*, *26*(1), 33–46.
Young, S. (2009). Towards constructions of musical childhoods: Diversity and digital technologies. *Early Child Development and Care*, *179*(6), 695–705.
Young, S. (2012a). Theorizing musical childhoods with illustrations from a study of girls' karaoke use at home. *Research Studies in Music Education*, *14*(2) 113–128.
Young, S. (2012b). MyPlace, MyMusic: An international study of musical experiences in the home among seven-year-olds. *Min-Ad: Israel Studies of Musicology Online*, *10*(1). Retrieved from http://www.biu.ac.il/hu/mu/min-ad/
Young, S. (2015). Imagining musical childhoods. *Perspectives: Journal of the Early Childhood Music and Movement Association*, *10*(1), 5–8.
Young, S., and Gillen, J. (2010). Musicality. In J. Gillen and C. A. Cameron (Eds.), *International perspectives on early childhood research: A day in the life* (pp. 59–76). Basingstoke, Hampshire: Palgrave Macmillan.
Young, S., and Ilari, B. (2012). Musical participation from birth to three: Towards a global perspective. In G. McPherson and G. Welch (Eds.), *Oxford handbook of music education*, vol. 1 (pp. 279–296). Oxford: Oxford University Press.
Young, S., Ilari, B., and Pérez, J. (2010). *MyPlace, MyMusic: An international study of children's everyday musical activities in diverse locations*. Paper presented at the

Twentieth European Early Childhood Education Research Association Conference (EECERA), Birmingham, UK.

Young, S., and Pérez, J. (2012). 'We-Research': Adopting a wiki to support the processes of collaborative research among a team of international researchers. *International Journal of Music Education, 30*(1), 3–17.

Young, S., Pérez, J., Addessi, A. R., Andang'o, E., Daugaard, S., Gluschankof, C., Holgersen, S., Ilari, B., Koutsoupidou, T., Leu, J., Lum, C., Mingher, F., Pacheco, C., Persellin, D., Retra, J. et al. (2010). MyPlace, MyMusic: An international study of musical experiences in the home among seven-year-olds. In B. Ilari and C. Gluschankof (Eds.), *Nurturing children's musical lives by building bridges. Proceedings of the 14th Early Childhood Music education Seminar of the International Society for Music Education* (pp. 61–65). Beijing: International Society for Music Education.

Zdzinski, S. F. (1996). Parental involvement, selected student attributes, and learning outcomes in instrumental music. *Journal of Research in Music Education, 44*(1), 34–48.

Contributors

Elizabeth Andang'o is Lecturer of Music Education in the Department of Music and Dance at Kenyatta University in Kenya. She teaches graduate courses in curriculum development in music education, pedagogy, and methods in music education. She also teaches voice, aural musicianship, and music appreciation at the undergraduate level. Her research interests include song and the development of singing from both physiological and cultural perspectives, multicultural music, curriculum development, psychology of music and pedagogy. She is also interested in all aspects of music in childhood (0–8 years), an area that is still quite novel in Kenya. She has presented research papers at Early Childhood Music Education Commission of the International Society for Music Education, and Research in Music Education (RIME) conferences among other forums. She is a team member in AMEP (African Music Education Project) undertaking research in Kenya, South Africa, and Zambia. She is also a team member in one of the projects under AIRS (Advancing Interdisciplinary Research in Music), a Canadian research initiative. She has published articles in *Arts Education Policy Research*, *Early Child Development and Care*, *Israeli Studies in Musicology Online*, and *East African Journal of Music Education*, among others. She is currently serving as Commissioner (2010–2016) in the Early Childhood Music Education Commission of the International Society of Music Education.

Claudia Gluschankof is Senior Lecturer at Levinsky College of Education, Tel-Aviv, where besides her teaching at the undergraduate and graduate levels in the Early Childhood Department and Music Department, she has served as a researcher at the Research and Development Authority and Coordinator of Studies at the School of Music (2002–2008). She holds an Orff certificate from the Orff Institute in Salzburg, Austria, and a Kodály certificate from the Kodály Institute in Kecskemét, Hungary. In addition to her teaching activity at the kindergarten level and teacher preservice and in-service training she served as member and head researcher of the Music Curriculum Committee of Israel. She served on the Early Childhood Music Education Commission (2006–2012, as chair 2008–2010) of the International Society for Music Education- Her research interests focus on the musical expressions of young children, particularly on self-initiated play of young children in various cultural contexts, especially among Hebrew and Arab speakers. Her research has been presented at many international conferences and published in various peer review journals.

Beatriz Ilari is Assistant Professor of Music Education at the University of Southern California (USC). Prior to her appointment at USC, she worked as Associate Professor of Music Education at the Federal University of Paraná in Brazil (2003–2010), and as the Lozano Long Visiting Associate Professor of Latin American Studies at the University of Texas in Austin. Her main research interests lie in the intersection between music, childhood, cognition, and culture. She is currently a research fellow at USC's Brain and Creativity Institute and a coinvestigator on the Advancing Interdisciplinary Research in Singing initiative. Her research has appeared in important journals such as the *Journal of Research in Music Education*, *Research Studies in Music Education*, *Early Child Development and Care*, Frontiers in Psychology, and the *Journal of Cross-Cultural Psychology*, to name a few. She has also published five books in Brazil, including *Música na infância e adolescência* and *Em busca da mente musical*. She is currently on the editorial board of the *Journal of Research in Music Education*, *Psychology of Music*, Musicae Scientiae, and *Research Studies in Music Education*. She is also the editor of *Perspectives: Journal of the Early Childhood Music and Movement Association*, and immediate past editor of the *International Journal of Music Education*.

Theano Koutsoupidou is Head of the School of Education at the Mediterranean College, Greece. She coordinates bachelor's and master's courses in Preschool and Special Education (in partnership with the University of Derby, UK) and delivers modules in research methods, teaching practice, and creativity. Her previous lecturing posts include the University of the Aegean, the University of Athens, the European University Cyprus, Vocational Training Institutes, secondary schools, and early childhood centers. She holds a Ph.D. in Music Education and a PGCE in Higher Education, both from the University of Surrey; a degree in Music Studies from the University of Athens; and degrees and diplomas in Piano and Clarinet performance. She is an active researcher and has widely presented and published her work. She has received awards from the European Society for Cognitive Sciences of Music (ESCOM), the Society for Education, Music and Psychology Research (SEMPRE), and the Greek Ministry of Education for her research contributions. She currently conducts research on musical play, funded by the Froebel Trust, UK. She is Fellow of the Higher Education Academy (FHEA), a former editorial board member of Arts Education Policy Review, and reviewer for major academic journals. Her research interests are in the fields of preschool music education, creativity, and child development.

Chee-Hoo Lum is Associate Professor of Music Education with the Visual and Performing Academic Group at the National Institute of Education (NIE), Nanyang Technological University, Singapore, and Head of UNESCO-NIE Centre for Arts Research in Education (CARE), part of a region-wide network of observatories stemming from the UNESCO Asia-Pacific Action Plan. His research interests include issues of identity, cultural diversity and multiculturalism, technology and globalization in music education; children's musical cultures; creativity and improvisation; and elementary music methods. He is currently a coeditor of the *International Journal of Music Education* and member of the editorial boards of *Research Studies in Music Education* and the *International Journal of Community Music*. He is a member of the steering committee of the International Network for Research in Arts Education and a board member of the Asia-Pacific Symposium for Music Education Research. He has previously been an associate editor with the *International Journal of Education and the Arts*. He has edited two books: *Contextualized Practices in Arts Education: An International Dialogue on Singapore* and *Musical Childhoods of Asia and the Pacific*, and has published school textbooks, academic book chapters, and refereed journal articles. He has also made numerous conference presentations at local and international venues.

Caroline Brendel Pacheco is Assistant Professor at the Federal University of Paraíba, where she has founded and directs a music education program for babies, toddlers, and young children. She is a Brazilian music educator, recorder player, and singer. She began her musical studies at the age of six at the School of Music and Fine Arts of Paraná (EMBAP) where she also studied piano and recorder. She holds a music licentiate degree from EMBAP and a master's degree in Music from the Federal University of Paraná. Her research focuses on early childhood music education, musical development, and the relationship between musical abilities and literacy.

Jèssica Pérez-Moreno is Lecturer at the Universitat Autònoma de Barcelona and a Visiting Research Associate at the Institute of Education, University of London. Her research interests are in the field of early childhood music education and focus on the use of technology and daily music situations. She is a member of the research group Música, Veu i Educació, recognized by the Department of Education of the Catalan government and also of the group Investigación en Educación Musical. She chaired the area of Music Education of the Multidisciplinary International Conference on Educational Research for the biennium 2013–2015 and is a member of the editorial boards of the two music education research journals published in Spain.

Diane Persellin is Professor and Coordinator of Music Education at Trinity University in San Antonio, Texas. She has served as Editor of General Music Today, President of Texas Music Educators Conference, Co-chair of the Mountain Lake Colloquium, and a Commissioner of Early Childhood Music Education (International Society for Music Education). Her publications include articles in *Journal of*

Research in Music Education, the *Bulletin of the Council of Research in Music Education*, *Update*, and *Journal of Scholarship in Teaching and Learning*. Her coauthored book, *A Concise Guide to Improving Student Learning*, was published by Stylus Press in 2014.

Sheila C. Woodward is Associate Professor and Chair of Music at Eastern Washington University. Cheney, Washington. She is a native of South Africa and has previously taught at the University of Southern California, the University of South Florida, and the University of the Western Cape. She is President of the International Society for Music Education (ISME) and serves on the editorial board of the *International Journal of Music Education*. Her research focus is Music and Wellbeing. She explores this from before birth to adulthood, with studies on the fetus, neonate, premature infant, young child, at-risk youth, juvenile offender, and adult musician. She has directed numerous outreach programs in both the United States and South Africa.

Susan Young is Retired Senior Lecturer in Early Childhood Studies and Music Education at the University of Exeter, UK. She is also Senior Research Fellow at the University of Roehampton, London, Associate of the Centre for Research in Early Childhood, Birmingham, and is affiliated with the University of Bristol, UK. In retirement she is now involved in overseas voluntary work at the university of Hargeisa, Somaliland. Her career has combined more than twenty years of university lecturing with a range of freelance research, evaluation, and consultancy specializing in early years arts, music, and education. Originally trained as a pianist at the Royal College of Music London, she went on to study Dalcroze Eurhythmics in Switzerland and the Kodály method in Hungary. She spent her early career teaching music in secondary and primary schools and in a range of early years settings. She has published widely in professional and academic journals and is frequently invited to present at conferences, both nationally and internationally. She has written several books, including *Music with the Under Fours* and *Music 3–5*.

Index

Italic page numbers refer to figures and tables.